THE WAY of LIFE SERIES

MARRIAGE
DIVORCE
and
PURITY

by

Joe D. Schubert

Published By
BIBLICAL RESEARCH PRESS
774 East North 15th Street
Abilene, Texas
79601

THE WAY of LIFE SERIES
MARRIAGE, DIVORCE, and PURITY
by

JOE D. SCHUBERT

CONTENTS

Lesson I

MARRIAGE IS FROM GOD

"There are two rocks in this world of ours, on which the soul must either anchor or be wrecked—the one is God, and the other is the sex opposite." [1] Marriage is solemn and glorious and there is no other earthly relationship that has so much power to ennoble and exalt, but, likewise, there are no more tragic consequences known to man than when the principles of marriage are perverted or abused.

Marriage originated in the mind of God Himself. Immediately after the creation of Adam, we read in Genesis 2:18-24:

> And Jehovah God said, It is not good that the man should be alone; I will make him a help meet for him. And out of the ground Jehovah God formed every beast of the field, and every bird of the heavens; and brought them unto the man to see what he would call them: and whatsoever the man called every living creature, that was the name thereof. And the man gave names to all cattle, and to the birds of the heavens, and to every beast of the field; but for the man there was not found a help meet for him. And Jehovah God caused a deep sleep to fall upon the man, and he slept; and he took one of his ribs, and closed up the flesh instead thereof: and the rib, which Jehovah God had taken from the man, made he a woman, and brought her unto the man. And the man said, This is now bone of my bones, and flesh of my flesh: she shall be called Woman, because she was taken out of Man. Therefore shall a man leave his father and his mother, and shall cleave unto his wife: and they shall be one flesh.

Thus, God, in the very beginning, created woman especially to be a companion for the man—to be a help meet (or suitable for) him. There can be no doubt that God intended for man and woman to marry, for He says, "For this cause shall a man leave his father and his mother, and shall cleave unto his wife." God "officiated" at this first marriage

---

[1] F. W. Robertson, 19th century English minister.

and He continues to officiate at all scriptural marriages today.

Marriage, then, is not something that was originated by man, or is a mere social custom. This is the reason we say that marriage is divine. Those who marry not only have obligations to each other, but they also have obligations to God. His will regarding marriage must be respected and obeyed.

There are many passages of the Scripture which show that it is God's will that men and women marry. In the New Testament, when Pharisees were questioning Jesus about marriage and divorce, he quoted from Genesis 2, and added: "What therefore *God hath joined* together, let not man put asunder" (Matt. 19:6). Jesus further gave his approval to marriage by His presence at the wedding feast in Cana of Galilee where he performed his first miracle (Jn. 2:1-11). The apostle Paul, guided by the Holy Spirit, compares the relationship between husband and wife to the relationship between Christ and his church (Eph. 5:22-25). Paul also exhorts the younger women "to marry, bear children, and guide the house" (I Tim. 5:14). He said further that those forbidding certain ones to marry were teaching "doctrines of demons" (I Tim. 4:1-3). Even one of the qualifications of elders and deacons is that they be the husband of one wife (I Tim. 3:3; 12; Titus 1:6). Some, however, have said that Paul actually disapproved of marriage because of what he said about it in I Corinthians 7. It is true that he did say some positive things there, but we need to fully understand the context of his remarks. The verses are 7-9:

> Yet I would that all men were even as I myself...I say to the unmarried and to widows, It is good for them if they abide even as I. But if they have not continency, let them marry: for it is better to marry than to burn.

Paul was not married, and when he urges others here to be like he was, some have thought he was condemning marriage. But this was the same Paul who exhorted younger women to marry and have children; who said that those forbidding to marry were teaching doctrines of demons; and who compared the relationship between husband and wife to that between Christ and the church. The key to a correct interpretation of these verses is found in verse 26: "I think therefore that this is good by reason of the distress that is upon us, namely, that it is good for a man to be as he is." Paul is saying this in view of the specially distressing times of those days—persecutions, etc.—it was better for a man not to marry, if he could control himself. But Paul made it plain that even in distressing times, it was not wrong to marry if there was a need for it: "But if thou marry, thou hast not sinned" (I Cor. 7:28). The testimony of all writers of the New Testament is summarized in the words of Heb. 13:4: "Let marriage be had in honor among all."

What are the basic purposes for marriage? The Bible suggests three main reasons why men and women should marry: (1) To provide companionship. Notice Gen. 2:18. God made the first woman to keep man from being lonely. The woman and the man complement each other; they fill each other's needs. Here, incidentally, is a wonderful manifestation of the love that God has for His creation. (2) To propagate the race. God blessed the first pair, and said to them, "Be fruitful, and multiply, and replenish the earth" (Gen. 1:28). The marriage union carries with it the high privilege, and obligation, of parenthood. Those who marry but who do not intend to have children will miss one of the greatest privileges that God has given to them. (3) To prevent immorality. Paul writes in I Cor. 7:2: "But because of fornications, let each man have his own wife, and let each woman have her own husband." God placed the sexual drive within each human being, and marriage is the arena in which He planned for this desire to be fulfilled. Paul teaches in I Cor. 7:3, 4 that the husband and wife have sexual *obligations* to each other, because neither has power over his own body; the wife has power over the husband and the husband over the wife. The act of sexual intercourse is considered as holy and proper within the marriage relationship, but intercourse outside of marriage is firmly condemned throughout the New Testament. Fornication and adultery are listed repeatedly in the several catalogues of sin found in the New Testament. It is through the institution of marriage that men and women are to protect themselves from fornication, and God intends that marriage be used to accomplish this purpose.

The restraints and limitations in God's guidebook were not intended to "take the pleasure out of life," but rather to put real pleasure and great satisfaction into life. God, who created man, knows which kind of experiences will best satisfy and which kind will not. For this reason God condemns the sex act outside of marriage. Those who flaunt and disregard God's restrictions will find that their choice of conduct does not bring true happiness. For instance, an outstanding New York City psychoanalyst, Dr. Eugene Eisner, tells of a patient who was not bound by religious restrictions in his sex life, and who reported that in ten years he had had six "love affairs." Yet his conclusion was, "I can't seem to enjoy any of it. Is there something the matter with me?" [2] Another psychiatrist states,

> For about fifteen years I have been the confidant of Broadway and Hollywood actors and actresses who have opportunities to live a promiscuous sexual life. And some of them live it to the hilt—eight, ten, twelve 'affairs' a year. But when they trust you and let down their hair, they will confess how frustrating and unsatisfying it all is. [3]

In a health clinic in San Francisco, two thousand girls who were in trouble were asked if they had received pleasure from their sexual experiences. According to the proponents of today's "new morality," we would expect an overwhelming enthusiastic "yes" from these girls. On the contrary, only one-third reported "some pleasure." The other two-thirds described their feelings as those of "doubt, guilt, shame, indifference, or definitely unpleasant." [4] All of this confirms again that greener pastures are never found by

[2] Maurice Zolotow, "Love is Not a Statistic," *Readers Digest,* April, 1954, p. 9.
[3] *Ibid.*
[4] Howard Whitman, "The Slavery of Sex Freedom," *Better Homes and Gardens,* June, 1957, p. 219.

breaking through God's fences. The inspired writer said long ago: "Let marriage be had in honor among all, and let the bed be undefiled: for fornication and adulterers God will judge" (Heb. 13:4).

We might ask, "What actually constitutes marriage?" Marriage, in God's sight, is the living together of a man and woman as husband and wife and involves two things: (1) The intention to be married. Two people who engage in sexual intercourse with no intention of being married to each other are not married; they merely commit fornication. If a young man were baptized, not with the intention of obeying Christ, but only to get his sweetheart to marry him, would he truly be united to Christ by that act? God will not join two people in marriage who do not desire in their hearts to be joined. (2) There must be a ceremony of some sort that is recognized and approved by the "powers that be"—by the government. In primitive times, this ceremony was no doubt very simple. But the accepted civil ceremony should be complied with. Thus, when two people love each other and desire to be with each other, and meet the civil requirements, they are husband and wife in God's sight.

Sexual intercourse is not required in order for a marriage to exist. The sexual union is a *privilege* of the marriage relationship, but it is not the act that forms or makes a marriage. By carefully reading Matthew 2:18-25, one can see that Joseph and Mary were considered husband and wife before they had engaged in sexual union. Verse 18 mentions that Mary was found to be with child "before they came together." This, in fact, is what puzzled Joseph, because he knew that the child she was carrying was not his. It had not yet been revealed to him that "that which is conceived in her is of the Holy Spirit." Yet, Joseph is called Mary's "husband" in verse 19, and the angel calls Mary his "wife" in verse 20. Joseph and Mary were husband and wife because they loved each other and desired to be with each other, and had evidently conformed to whatever ceremonies were required. The sexual union occurred later. Matthew says he "knew her not till she had brought forth a son." (verse 25). The word "knew" in the Bible sometimes means to have intercourse, and signifies "carnal" knowledge.

A marriage is recognized by God, then, when a man and woman resolve in their hearts to live together as husband and wife, and conform to a proper civil ceremony. If a man and woman have not made this resolve, no number of civil ceremonies can join them. There is no middle ground between marriage and fornication. Two people who are living together are either married or they are committing fornication. There is no other choice.

If marriage is seen only as a means of satisfying the sex urge, man places himself on the level of an animal. The sex instincts are God-given; hence, sex is not a shameful or vulgar thing to be spoken about in whispers. But the Bible teaches us that it takes much more than the physical to make a marriage. Dr. S. I. McMillen, in his recent book, *None of These Diseases,* puts the point well when he says:

> The password to a happy marriage is *together*—live together, play together, work together, think together, and plan together. Two people can not be held together long unless there is some sort of binding force, and sexuality is a short-lived binder, as the sex marriages of Hollywood have long demonstrated. Because sex is the only cohesive that many couples know anything about, it is not strange that about one out of every three marriages falls apart. [5]

Christian marriage is a wonderful and beautiful thing. Through it, men and women cooperate with God in fulfilling the high destinies to which they have been called. The husband and the wife, in learning to love, come to a fuller understanding of that great love which Christ has for His church. Thus, we can come to know God through our homes as well as through the church.

---

[5] S. I. McMillen, *None of These Diseases* (Westwood, N. J.: Spire Books, Fleming H. Revell Co., 1963), p. 53.

QUESTIONS FOR LESSON I

1. What Scriptures would you use to show a person that marriage is not something that has simply "evolved" in the history of man, but that it originated with God himself?

2. What do you know about the "distress" that is referred to by Paul in I Cor. 7:26? Why would it have been better for a Christian not to have been married while those conditions prevailed?

3. Discuss our need for companionship. Is this really one of man's *basic* needs?

4. What would you say to a young couple who are planning to be married, but who say they don't want any children?

5. Discuss these two statements:
    "Sex is sinful."
    "There are sinful uses of sex."

6. What examples can you cite which show that God's restrictions are for our good and that to ignore them brings unhappiness?

7. Comment on this statement: "Man-made laws cannot join a man and woman in marriage any more than man-made laws can dissolve a marriage."

8. Is pre-marital sexual intercourse wrong for two young people who are planning to be married later? Why? Does the sexual act make them married?

Lesson II

PREPARATION FOR MARRIAGE

Suppose you were planning to drive to a certain resort area for a vacation. Suppose you were told that on the road to this place were the most dangerous traffic hazards in the world; that one out of every three automobiles traveling this road had a wreck; that the casualties in broken lives ran into the millions! I am sure you would weigh every consideration carefully before you deliberately undertook such a hazardous journey. You no doubt recognize this road as the "highway of marriage" on which one out of every three couples is wrecked by divorce. The startling fact is that experts can predict with a high degree of accuracy which marriages will be wrecked! Some marriages can be known to be practically doomed before they start. Wrong people marry, for the wrong purposes, with the wrong motives, and with wrong preparation.

There are many false ideas about marriage. Most people take for granted that love is the only thing that really counts in marriage. Motion pictures, novels, and advertisements all hammer this idea home. The argument is that love is a strange, mysterious something which nobody can understand, and there doesn't seem to be anything anyone should do to control it. But an inescapable fact is that each year thousands of bitter and disillusioned couples, who were once quite as much in love with each other as most young people are at the time of marriage, crowd our divorce courts. Obviously, something has gone wrong. For some reason, the love that once was so powerful, has not continued. This suggests that selecting life partners solely on the basis of this supposed "love feeling" is not enough.

A successful marriage is in great measure the result of the preparation that has been made for it...physically, morally, intellectually, vocationally, emotionally, spiritually. The period of courtship offers the opportunity for this preparation. It takes time and effort to grow up to have the ideals and faith and character someone else should want. And yet this is the price of a happy, lasting marriage.

Physical preparation. A strong, healthy body is a wonderful asset to a happy marriage. Illness and physical weakness often put severe strains on marriage, even to the breaking point. A sincere effort should be made to avoid habits such as smoking, drinking, and any others that are harmful to the body. Paul warns that if we engage in those things which destroy or harm our body, God will destroy us (I Cor. 3:16, 17).

Moral preparation. There is no substitute for moral purity. Some claim that premarital sex relationships are helpful to good marriage adjustment. But the truth is, that far from being valuable, they could easily prove to be very detrimental. They can often ruin what otherwise might develop into a happy and successful marriage. Dr. Wayne Anderson, in his *Design for Family Living,* states positively that

> There is no definitive research which substantiates the thinking that premarital intercourse will improve a couple's relationship. On the other hand, there are sound studies which suggest that the couple's relationship tends to deteriorate when coitus (intercourse) is engaged in before marriage.... One study found that those who engaged in premarital intercourse had a higher percentage of divorces than those who did not. [6]

Of course, the real issue for the Christian young person is that such a practice, in addition to being a sin against himself and the one he loves, is also a sin against God. Purity and honor are a very real part of the Christian ideal as one comes to maturity and prepares for marriage. God's word puts it bluntly; "Thou shalt not commit adultery" (Rom. 13:9).

Intellectual preparation. The higher the educational level, the greater the chance for success in marriage. [7] If you finish high

---

[6] Minneapolis: T. S. Denison & Co., 1964, p. 80, 81.
[7] Sylvanus M. Duvall, *Before You Marry* (New York: Association Press, 1949), p. 37.

school before you marry, your chance for a permanent marriage is greater than if you don't. If you finish college, your chance of staying married longer and more happily is greater than if you don't. There are strong arguments which deny wisdom in teenage marriages. "A study of 60 teen-age brides in Iowa showed that 55 per cent regretted marrying before completing high school."[8] Furthermore, such a marriage has little chance of lasting. One study of marriage in a certain high school showed that "among 240 married couples...(where one or both mates dropped out of school to marry) only sixteen couples were still living together after five years."[9] One sociologist reports that "the divorce rate for those who marry in their teens is six times as high as that in any other age group."[10]

It would be unthinkable to put an immature and un-trained person into the cockpit of a jet and expect him to take off and fly to a destination. Yet every day teen-agers are attempting to take over the controls of a marriage for which they have little or no training. Someone has suggested the following reasons why teen-agers are too young to marry:

(a) Marriage is serious business and there is much more to being serious than simply the wish or desire. Teen-agers cannot have enough knowledge about marriage to really be serious about it.
(b) Teenagers have not yet really learned to live with themselves.
(c) Too often boys do not realize they are trying to find a shortcut to manhood by assuming outward signs, one of which is marriage.
(d) Teenagers cannot promise to be steadfast, true and constant to another human being because they are not really in a position to keep that promise. Their

[8] "Survey Bulletin," Baptist Sunday School Board, Nashville, Tennessee, Feb. 17, 1961.
[9] Earl H. Hanson, "Teen-age Marriages," NEA Journal, Sept., 1961, p. 27.
[10] Wayne Anderson, Design for Family Living (Minneapolis: T. S. Denison & Co., 1964), p. 35.

growth, development and education are all incomplete. They are still in the midst of the transformation which changes a child into a man or woman.

(e) Persons mature physically before they mature in character. One is not fully himself until he is past twenty years of age.

(f) Ten years later, the teenager will not be at all the same kind of person he or she is now. This means that today's teenager is not in position to pick the mate for the adult he or she will soon become.

Vocational preparation. Are you preparing yourself to take on the financial responsibility of marriage? "Two can live as cheaply as one," provided one doesn't eat, dress, get sick, or care to go out anywhere. Studies have found that "invariably the successful, happy marriages were characterized by an adequate income from the start."[11] Researchers have also found that with the larger percentage of happy couples, the wife does not work.[12] The husband is the breadwinner and the wife is the homemaker. Most authorities agree that the working-wife situation poses a difficult psychological adjustment for both. The husband has a need to feel pride in his masculine role, and this pride is threatened when the wife must help earn the income.

Above all, one should not cut short his educational or vocational preparation to get married. The handwriting is on the wall in letters ten feet high that there is little chance of a decent economic future for the unskilled or untrained person in tomorrow's society. Without at least a high school education (and in most cases, without a college education), a man is destined for the lower paying jobs or the dullest of occupations. He can expect to periodically find himself in the ranks of the unemployed. The jobs of the next decade will demand education and training on a scale never before approached in the United States. When one cuts his education short, he may be sentencing himself, his mate,

---

[11] Wayne Dehoney, *Homemade Happiness* (Nashville: Broadman Press, 1963) p. 42.
[12] *Ibid.*

and his children to a prison house of continuous poverty, want, financial insecurity, and lack of opportunity.

Emotional preparation. Emotional growth and maturity are imperative. One of the chief causes of failure in marriage is emotional immaturity on the part of one of the partners. Adams suggests the following indications or tests for genuine emotional maturity:

(a) You should be able to carry a reasonable load of emotional tension without blowing up. When you face annoyances and disappointments, frustrations, or difficulties, you must be able to face them without going to pieces, or getting sulky, or refusing to speak, or resorting to other silly, childish ways so often seen in the immature.

(b) You should have outgrown childish and foolish fears and anxieties, e.g. fear of the dark or of being alone. Young people are sometimes afraid of being different or of standing up for their own convictions.

(c) Learn to expect to be treated as a responsible partner in marriage. "Some men want to be mothered and waited on all their lives instead of taking a man's place in the home as well as in society. Too often a woman expects just a delightful and continuing courtship and wants to be babied and cared for all the time, instead of getting down to the stern realities of making a home and rearing a family." Each must be ready to carry his share of the load and develop the skills that will make this possible.

(d) "You should be emotionally independent of your parents and able to stand on your own feet and make your own decisions in life." Included in this is the ability to look plainly at your own faults and limitations and seek to correct them. The ability to bear the responsibilities of fatherhood and motherhood is also involved. If you marry, you may have a baby within a year, whether you plan it that way or not. [13]

Spiritual preparation. Are you a faithful Christian? This includes regular church attendance, but very much more. Read the Sermon on the Mount (Matt. 5, 6, 7). This out-

---

[13] Theodore F. Adams, *Making Your Marriage Succeed* (New York: Harper & Bros., 1953), pp. 33, 34.

lines some demands of the spiritual life. How do you measure up? Especially notice what Christ says about forgiveness (Matt. 6:14, 15). Are you capable of forgiving? When two imperfect partners in an imperfect world are bound together in an imperfect human relationship, they both must be able to forgive "seventy times seven." The finest guarantee for a happy and lasting marriage is for both partners to be spiritually minded, faithful Christians, and dedicated to Jesus Christ and to His cause.

Many passages in the Scriptures deal with the responsibilities which rest upon the husband and wife in the marriage relationship.

Notice some verses dealing with the husband's responsibility to the wife. Eph. 5:23: "For the husband is the head of the wife, as Christ also is the head of the church." God has decreed that the head of the family is to be the man. He exercises his headship by "living considerately with your wives, bestowing honor on the woman as the weaker sex...in order that your prayers may not be hindered" (I Pet. 3:7, RSV).

The husband must love his wife. "Husbands, love your wives, even as Christ also loved the church, and gave himself up for it" (Eph. 5:25).

The husband is to honor his wife. "Ye husbands...give honor unto the woman as unto the weaker vessel" (I Pet. 3:7). How does the husband give honor? As the RSV puts it, by "living considerately" with his wife. An inconsiderate husband is one who does not honor his wife, and thus violates God's commands. Sympathy, understanding, tenderness and affection are all a part of honor.

The husband has the responsibility of supporting his wife. Paul states that if a man does not provide for his own family, he is worse than an infidel (I Tim. 5:8). Whether due to laziness, shiftlessness, drunkenness, or whatever, if a man fails to provide for his family, he has committed a serious sin against God.

There are also passages dealing with the wife's duties in the marriage relationship. In most marriage ceremonies, the bride promises to "love, honor, and obey" her husband. These three words pinpoint the wife's major responsibilities, according to the Scriptures.

She is to love her husband (Titus 2:4). Here again, a practical application of I Corinthians 13 is the ideal. The marriage union is based on a foundation of mutual love between the husband and wife.

The wife is to respect or honor her husband. "Let the wife see that she respects her husband." (Eph. 5:33, RSV). This involves a respect for his wishes, his tastes, and appreciation of his efforts, and an encouragement of him in those things which are right.

The wife is to be in submission to her husband. "Wives, be in subjection to your husbands, as is fitting in the Lord" (Col. 3:18). (See also Eph. 5:22 and I Peter 3:1.) The only way the husband can be the head of his home (Eph. 5:23) is for the wife to submit to his rule.

The attitudes we take into marriage have much to do with its success. If marriage is treated lightly, then we are not likely to work at it very hard. Some view marriage as some sort of experiment. They say, "Let's try it and if we don't like it we'll get a divorce." The chances of this type marriage ever succeeding are very slim. God intends for each person entering marriage to do so with the intention of living with that mate until death. His pattern is: One man for one woman for life. For the Christian, the concept of marriage as an "experiment" is simply out of bounds.

At times, a young person may marry out of love for what the other person can do for him. This type of love is actually only a form of selfishness. This kind of "love" should be taken as a warning signal rather than as a basis for marriage.

There are also some who marry hoping to reform and re-make the one they think they love. They are actually in love with what their mate can become rather than in love with the mate as he is. Some of these persons tend to feel that, after marriage, the mate will automatically become a perfect person. But human beings are human beings after marriage, just as before. The chances are that a person will be the same after the vows are read as he was before.

When two young people enter into marriage with such false notions or misconceptions, all the signs point to rough sledding ahead. "If marriage is to find its meaning and fulfill its purpose we must marry...with unselfish love, each loving the other for what he or she is, and thinking of what each can do to bring out the best in each other."[14]

The maturity that one needs in order to be a good hus-band or wife comes only through continued growth. One of the most difficult tasks of ministers and marriage counselors is to persuade people to take time, time to grow, time to find the right person, time to fall in love intelligently and completely, and time to become the right person. In the faith and fellowship of the church you can find the kind of person you want to marry, and there you can grow to be the person someone else will want. As you grow in other ways, be sure to grow in your understanding of what God can mean in your life. Learn the privilege and power of prayer. Study God's Word and build its truth and ideals and principles into your daily life. Grow as Jesus grew "in wisdom and stature, and in favor with God and men" (Lk. 2:52). With two such lives, you and God together can build an enduring, happy, and successful home.

---

[14] P. D. Wilmeth, "Why Many Marriages Fail," *Gospel Advocate,* June 30, 1960.

QUESTIONS FOR LESSON II

1. It is sometimes said that love can surmount any barrier. Is this true?

2. Discuss some real problems that can arise in one's marriage as a result of poor health of either the husband or the wife.

3. Suggest some reasons why premarital sex relations may cause poor adjustment in marriage.

4. Why do you suppose the divorce rate among teen-age marriages is so high?

5. Discuss the reasons listed why teenagers are too young to marry. Do you think they are valid?

6. Suppose two high school students were planning to be married during the summer, between their junior and senior years. Would you encourage them in these plans? Why?

7. Relate some instances of emotional immaturity you have observed in married couples.

8. In what respect is the husband the head of the wife?

9. Mention some ways in which a husband can dishonor his wife—and ways in which a wife can fail to show proper respect for her husband.

10. Discuss the following false concepts of marriage:
    (a) Marriage is an experiment
    (b) Marriage for what the other person can do for you
    (c) Marriage with the hope of reforming your mate

Lesson III
SELECTING A MARRIAGE PARTNER

A local businessman once printed the following in white chalk on his grocery store window: "Wanted—a wife, 18-21. Must have teeth—Bachelor grocer." This was done as a gag to attract business. To the owner's amazement, forty-one girls phoned to inquire about the ad. Two proposed over the phone. One girl mailed an offer of marriage. Three came into the store to present themselves as possible marriage partners.

Obviously, this is not a very sensible way to choose a mate, yet many people seek a husband or wife in equally ridiculous manners. Advertising one's desire to marry, wooing a girl who will inherit a fortune, or trapping a football star are methods engaged in by some who do not understand the challenge of marriage.

There is an old saying that "likes repel and opposites attract." But such a broad generalization might easily be carried to ridiculous extremes. If opposites attract, then the intelligent should marry morons, large persons should marry small ones, college students should marry illiterates, etc. If likes repel, similar interests, values, temperaments, or backgrounds would produce discord in marriage rather than harmony. The truth is that husbands and wives should have complementary rather than clashing characteristics.

It is the consensus of all studies that the more a man and woman have in common, the more stable and happy their marriage will be. Experts have even gone so far as to "scientifically match" couples with unbelievable success. The Scientific Marriage Foundation, of Mellott, Indiana, receives applications from persons desiring to meet eligible prospective mates. Applicants fill out a detailed form on background, interests, expectations of a mate which is verified by a local minister or counselor before it is mailed in. This information is transferred to IBM cards which are then scientifically matched. Then total strangers who are matched in common interests and background are put in contact with each other through the Foundation. Many of these "scientifically matched" couples have met and married and so far there is less than a one per cent divorce rate among them. Would these unbelievable statistics indicate that IBM matched mating will someday replace "moonlight and roses" romance as a prelude to marriage? We hope not! But the implications are inescapable—a successful marriage is directly related to how well two people are matched in their basic interests.

It is so important that one marry a right person. Notice we did not say *the* right person, but *a* right person. The idea that there is just one right person for you is nonsense. Actually there are probably many persons with whom you could be happily married. But these will all be people who are suitable for you in a number of significant respects. What are some of the factors, then, which should be considered in selecting a marriage partner?

Does he or she have real character? Character is the only real basis upon which a successful Christian marriage can be built. There is no substitute for it. The person who has "pep" and "vivaciousness" is undoubtedly attractive to the opposite sex. He or she gives promise of fun and gaiety, and we all like that. Certainly fun and a sense of humor make no one ineligible as a partner in a happy marriage, but let those qualities be the meringue, and see that there is something substantial underneath. Remember this is the person with whom you're going to share all things in your life—the little things as well as the big. This is the person who will be the mother or father of your children. Charm, wealth, popularity, or beauty will never be able to take the place of genuine character. Solomon describes a woman with real character in Proverbs 31. Read his description.

Is he or she sympathetic and considerate? Sympathy, in the literal sense, is a feeling for and with someone else—an understanding and consideration for the other person. Hard, rigid, uncompromising people can be very efficient, but very poor marriage partners.

Does he or she have a cheerful philosophy of life? The person whose philosophy of life includes generous impulses toward people and things is the one that you should single out as possibly good marriage material. A ready smile, a friendly cordiality toward life and people in general—these are some of the outward expressions of a cheerful philosophy. The person who walks into a new house and sees only the cracks in the ceiling or the paint that needs retouching is the same person who will be a continual fault finder whenever people or things fail to measure up to a certain standard.

Don't link your life with someone who is overly critical. At first you may feel flattered that such a super-being has shown favor to you, but don't be misled. In time you, too, will be a squirming specimen under the microscope of this relentless perfectionist.

Is he or she physically attractive? Of course you want to be proud of the appearance of the person you marry; that goes without saying. But what do we mean by physical attractiveness? A Zulu with a nose ring would not qualify in America, but according to jungle standards she might be a glamour girl. After all, beauty is largely a matter of social custom. It is important, however, that the mate you choose be physically attractive to you. This factor cannot be safely disregarded. But there are other factors which are just as important. Most men and women are married to persons whose looks fall somewhat short of the classic beauty of Venus or Apollo, yet they are very happy in their relationships. Increasing age is bound to have some effect on youthful appearance. There are so many aspects of marriage just as important as the physical that it is essential not to lose sight of them.

Recent studies in psychology have indicated that sex can be continuously satisfying only if it involves the response of total personalities to each other. [15] Otherwise, men will soon tire of women, no matter how beautiful they are. If you are a girl whom men find unusually attractive, you have a special problem at this point. It will be difficult for both you and them to know whether what they feel toward you is merely sexual attraction, or more genuine attraction that is deep enough and substantial enough on which to build a marriage. Your best safeguard is the character and integrity of the man.

In short, look for attractiveness—yes! But be sure it is more than skin deep. The English poet Oliver Goldsmith once said, "I chose my wife as she did her wedding gown, for qualities that would wear well." The Scriptures teach us that the heart of a person is so much more important than the outward appearance. (Cf. I Sam. 16:7; Prov. 23:7).

Does he or she have good health? No person who falls in love is going to come calling with a corsage in one hand and a stethoscope in the other to see if his date is physically fit. But with all facetiousness aside, whenever you select the person with whom you are going to spend the rest of your life, you should consider the importance of good health. It may not enhance the case for romance, but before you select your mate consider these facts about a marriage with someone who is in poor health: (a) There may be no children from such a union, and for most people that point is a vital consideration. (b) If there are children, they may inherit tendencies to physical weakness. (c) Medical care may be a severe financial strain. (d) The husband and wife may lack that social and sexual companionship which plays an important part in happy marriages. (e) A husband or wife's health affects not only themselves, but their entire family. It can affect one's entire outlook on life. The roles of husbands and wives are heavy, and it will be difficult to fulfill them well without good health.

All of this is not to say that marriages cannot be happy

---

[15] Duvall, *op. cit.,* p. 13.

where sickness exists. Sometimes an unusually beautiful relationship can grow out of such a condition, but the chances for establishing a happy normal home are greater if both husband and wife are strong and healthy. Think of this in selecting your mate.

Does he or she have emotional control? A pretty, fragile, clinging vine may be charming as a sweetheart, but in a wife you want a woman able to face the realities of life without tears and wailing and nervous breakdowns. A stormy, tempestuous lover may make your heart beat faster, but in a husband you want a man mature enough to face difficulties without flying into a rage. Child wives and spoiled boys belong at home with mother; they are not grown up enough to face marriage. In other words, do not marry an emotional adolescent. Try to fall in love with someone whose ideals, interests, and emotional reactions approach maturity. You will lead a much happier life.

Do you have similar interests? As we stated earlier, it has been said that opposites attract, but if people vary too much in their basic tastes, there may be trouble ahead. A certain number of similar interests is a must. In one sense, similar interests suggest such things as hobbies, sports, and cultural tastes. It is important that couples have some such interests in common. Do you enjoy similar books and similar ways of spending your leisure time? It is also important that they also have individual interests, for these may add stimulation and zest to the relationship. It is not necessary that husband and wife have the *same* interests, but it is necessary that whatever interests each one has, they are acceptable to the other. When such interests are not mutually acceptable, they may drive a couple apart instead of drawing them together. A hobby may be an intruder instead of a binder.

The term "similar interests" may also signify common purposes, goal, ideals, similar interpretations of life in general, similar attitudes toward such important things as children, home, religion, values, sex, people, money, property. It is apparent without explanation how profoundly significant such common interests are in marriage.

Do you have similar backgrounds? On one point practically all studies of success in marriage agree: The more similar their background, the greater chance a couple will have for success and the easier and happier will be their adjustments. [16] There are simply fewer opportunities for clashes between the husband and wife if they are of the same race, are accustomed to the same standard of living, and have similar educational and social backgrounds. Your own group may not be better than other groups, but it is more than likely better for you.

Perhaps a note should be added here concerning interracial marriages. In America there seems to be more intermixture of races than there is intermarriage among them. This is due partly to legal restrictions, since it is unlawful in some states for persons of different races to marry each other. A great barrier to interracial marriage lies in the established customs of the society and its negative attitudes toward such marriages. This attitude limits the number of intermarriages and makes it extremely difficult for those which do occur. In the United States, the least acceptable variety of interracial marriage is that between white and Negro. With public opinion as it is, the odds are great against such a marriage producing happiness. What is true of Negro-white marriages is true to a lesser degree of all interracial marriages. There are instances of success, but such instances are in the minority. Marriage always gives rise to a number of problems, but in many interracial marriages the problems have a good chance of proving fatal.

What about the family? It is true that you are not marrying a family, but it is a simple fact that, whether you want it that way or not, the wedding delivers to each of you free of charge a complete set of in-laws. These in-laws will visit and be visited, will make demands of one sort or another, and in many cases, will try to hold you to their own pattern of life. Much depends upon how close you are to them geographically, but geography does not always erase family

---

[16] *Ibid.,* p. 49.

bonds or release a person from the patterns of life that have been woven around him. If you are not compatible with your mate's family, there will probably be rough sledding ahead.

Are you close enough to each other in age? In most marriages, the man is somewhat older, for well-known reasons. Girls usually mature physically and socially from two to three years sooner than boys. Men feel the need to be able to provide for a wife financially before proposing marriage whereas women, not being expected to earn the family living, feel free to marry earlier. Studies have found that the happiest couples are those in which the husband is from three to five years older than the wife.[17]

Do you really love each other? Love is one of the most abused words in the English language. Consider each of the following uses of the word:

> "But now abideth faith, hope, *love,* these three and the greatest of these is love." (I Cor. 13:13).

> "See it now! Uncensored! *Love* in the raw!"

> "I just *love* that hat. Isn't it absolutely divine?"

> "Do you promise to *love,* honor, and obey?"

> "Aw, come on—just this once—prove your *love.*"

> "I *love* strawberries, but they give me a rash."

> "Hereby know we *love,* because he laid down his life for us: and we ought to lay down our lives for the brethren" (I John 3:16).

What really is love: Paul vividly describes the type of love on which a marriage should be built in I Corinthians 13. Here is how that chapter reads in J. B. Phillip's translation:

---

[17] *Ibid.,* p. 29.

This love of which I speak is slow to lose patience. It looks for a way of being constructive. It is not possessive. It is neither anxious to impress nor does it cherish inflated ideas of its own importance. Love has good manners and does not pursue selfish advantages. It is not touchy. It does not compile statistics of evil or gloat over the wickedness of other people. On the contrary, it is glad with all good men when truth prevails. Love knows no limit to its endurance; no end to its trust; no failing of its hope. It can outlast anything. It is in fact, the one thing that still stands when all else is fallen.

Too many young people confuse genuine love with infatuation. Someone has put it this way:

Infatuation may come at first sight, but love takes time. Infatuation may be based on sex alone, but real love includes many traits. Infatuation often means just being in love with love. Love means being in love with another person. Infatuation may be purely selfish, but love is unselfish. The physical element is more important in infatuation. The spiritual element is more important in love. Infatuation may change overnight, but love lasts. [18]

Actually, we do not *fall* into love; we grow into it. It is possible that you may "fall in love" several times before you marry. But you cannot erase the harm done to your own life, to another, and to your children, if you let an infatuation plummet you into a wrong marriage. God's Word teaches that genuine love underlies all successful God-approved marriages. Read thoughtfully Ephesians 5:25-33.

The time element. A valid type of love takes time to develop. You just can't meet a person one night, then marry, and expect to be happy. There are rare cases, of course, where hasty marriages have proved happy, but they are the exception rather than the rule. Really coming to know a person takes time, and lots of it. Sometimes young people ask, "Just how long should an engagement be?" The only

---

[18] As quoted by M. Norvel Young, "The Christian Home," *Firm Foundation,* Jan. 26, 1965.

answer that can be given to this question is that it all depends on how long you have known each other and how well you were acquainted before you became engaged. Several studies indicate that happiness in marriage is directly related to the length of engagement.[19] These same studies indicate that those couples who have been engaged for two years or longer are most successful in their marriages.[20] One authority recommends: "It seems logical...to conclude that the average couple should be engaged at least six months or longer according to the length of time needed to make the proper preparation for marriage."[21]

In an attempt to get at the personality traits which make for happiness or unhappiness in marriage, one sociologist asked 792 couples to rank the most common grievances each mate had against the other according to their seriousness in causing difficulty in the marriage. The top ten grievances listed by husbands and wives appear as follows:[22]

Order Listed by Husbands
1. Wife nags me.
2. Wife not affectionate.
3. Wife selfish and inconsiderate.
4. Wife complains too much.
5. Wife interferes with my hobbies.
6. Wife slovenly in appearance.
7. Wife is quick-tempered.
8. Wife interferes with my discipline.
9. Wife conceited.
10. Wife is insincere.

Order Listed by Wives
1. Husband selfish and inconsiderate.
2. Husband unsuccessful in business.
3. Husband is untruthful.
4. Husband complains too much.
5. Husband does not show affection.

---

[19] Anderson, *op. cit.,* p. 93.
[20] *Ibid.*
[21] *Ibid.*
[22] Judson and Mary Landis, *Personal Adjustment, Marriage and Family Living,* 3rd ed. (Englewood Cliffs, N. J.: Prentice-Hall, Inc., 1960), p. 292.

6. Husband does not talk things over.
7. Husband harsh with children.
8. Husband touchy.
9. Husband has no interest in children.
10. Husband not interested in home.

You will notice that the large majority of these traits are not traits that develop suddenly after marriage. Most of them were present before marriage, but the future husband or wife was blind to them, or else did not consider them serious enough to cause difficulty in their marriage. Another study of a large number of couples who had been successfully married for some years revealed that these couples explained their success in marriage on the basis of certain personality traits. They mentioned most often: affection, understanding, ability to give and take, cooperation, and willingness to talk things over. More care in choosing a marriage partner could go a long way toward ensuring the success of marriage.

There is a danger that, in making lists of characteristics to consider in choosing a mate, we will leave the impression that one should not marry until he finds the perfect person. We must be realistic and accept the fact that no one is perfect. Benjamin Tillett once said, "God help the man who won't marry until he finds a perfect woman, and God help him still more if he finds her."

The things which have been discussed in this lesson are vitally important. Use all the guidance you can in choosing a mate. But once you are married, try earnestly to do what you can toward making your marriage a grand success, regardless of the shortcomings of you or your mate. Try to build your relationship into the kind that will have the approval of God.

QUESTIONS FOR LESSON III

1. Discuss the implications of "scientifically matched" marriages.

2. How would you define "character"?

3. Enumerate the graces of character mentioned in Proverbs 31.

4. Why is "sympathy" an essential quality in a marriage partner?

5. What is a "perfectionist"? Why would such a person be a poor choice for marriage?

6. Have you ever known a beautiful girl or a handsome boy who were unattractive to you? Why were they? Have you ever known one who was not "good-looking" but who was very attractive to you? Why were they?

7. In what ways could poor health handicap a marriage?

8. What would be some indications that a person is able to control his emotions?

9. Think of some concrete examples of how a husband and wife can be driven apart because of conflicting interests.

10. What is your attitude toward interracial marriages?

11. Names some problems which are likely to arise in marriage if there is too much age difference between the partners.

12. Names some things you cannot learn about a person without knowing a person for a relatively long period of time.

Lesson IV

MIXED MARRIAGES

In the last lesson, an additional question, which must be answered in the process of selecting a marriage partner, was omitted deliberately because an entire lesson needs to be devoted to it. It is this: *Is he or she a faithful Christian?*

Your partner's spiritual life is more important than any of the physical and mental characteristics discussed in lesson three. In fact, since marriage is essentially a spiritual relationship, a common religious faith is the surest foundation upon which to establish a successful marriage. Religion is not something that can be pigeonholed and brought out only when convenient. Every crisis will bring religious faith to the forefront.

Religion can be a source of strength in marriage, but it can also become a storm center of conflict that separates instead of unifying. Psychologists and sociologists are unanimous in their testimony that religious differences can be one of the most divisive factors in marriage. A "Mixed Marriage" as used in this lesson, is a marriage in which the husband and wife are members of different churches.

Dehoney states the problem well in these words:

"As young people of different religious backgrounds are mixed together by these changing social patterns they tend to ignore or minimize their religious difference. Religious belief is reduced to the lowest common denominator. Sometimes merely a vague belief in God is considered an adequate faith. They find each other socially attractive, they date, they fall in love, and then marry. They are relatively free to do this, for parents today have very little to say about whom their child may date or may choose to marry. Furthermore, the popular concept is that love and romance, spelled with capital letters and embroidered in lace, will overcome all the problems of marriage! Then one day the couple finds their marriage filled with tensions and hostilities that seem impossible to resolve because of conflicting religious beliefs and loyalties." [23]

A marriage between people of different beliefs is fraught with all kinds of difficulties. It is a noble desire to want to win one's mate to Christ. But the hard fact of the matter is that there is no assurance that the one who cannot be won before marriage will be won after marriage! God did not intend for marriage to serve as a basic means of missionary work!

When "Mixed Marriages" are mentioned, we automatically think of marriages between a Catholic and a non-Catholic. Such a marriage is beset with almost insurmountable difficulties. The partners to the marriage must choose whether they will marry in the Catholic Church or outside it. If they decide to be married by a priest, both parties to the wedding must sign an official "Antenuptial Agreement" in the presence of the priest who will read the vows. The non-Catholic agrees to have all his children reared in the Catholic faith. The couple also agrees to have no other marriage ceremony before or after the Catholic service. A copy of this agreement is:

ANTE-NUPTIAL AGREEMENT [24] *

To Be Signed by Applicants for Dispensation from Impediment of Mixed Religion or Disparity of Cult

NON-CATHOLIC PARTY

I, the undersigned _____ of _____ not a member of the Catholic Church, desiring to contract marriage with _____ of ____ who is a member of the Catholic Church, propose to do so with the understanding that

---

[23] Dehoney, *op. cit.*, p. 49.

[24] Landis, *op. cit.*, p. 184. *Though we are aware that the Second Vatican Council, 1962-1965, has liberalized many Catholic teachings and requirements, including their attitude toward other faiths, we should remember that it is still the same church that stipulated all these restrictions, and that it still has very rigid views.

the marriage bond thus contracted can be broken only by death.

And thereupon in consideration of such marriage, I, the said_____, do hereby covenant, promise, and agree to and with the said_____that he (she), the said _____according to the Catholic faith without hindrance or adverse comment and that all the children of either sex born of such marriage, shall be baptized and educated only in the faith and according to the teachings of the Roman Catholic Church, even if the said_____ shall die first.

I hereby promise that no other marriage ceremony than that by the Catholic priest shall take place.

I furthermore realize the holiness of the use of marriage according to the teaching of the Catholic Church which condemns birth control and similar abuses of marriage. I shall have due respect for the religious principles and convictions of my Catholic partner.

Witness my hand this_____day of_____, 19____at _____ in the County of _____and State of

Signed in the presence of
Rev. _____

_____
Signature of non-Catholic

CATHOLIC PARTY

I, the undersigned_____, a member of the Catholic Church, of _____ Parish,_____wishing solemnly promise to have all the children of either sex born of this marriage baptized and reared only in the Catholic faith.

Furthermore, I promise that no other marriage ceremony than that by the Catholic priest shall take place.

I also realize my obligation in conscience to practice my religion faithfully and prudently to endeavor by prayer, good example, and the reception of the Sacraments, to induce my life partner to investigate seriously the teachings of the Catholic Church in the hope that such investigation may lead to conversion.

Witness my hand this _____ day of _____, 19 at _____ in the County of _____ and State of_____.

Signed in the presence of
Rev. _____

Signature of Catholic

For a Christian young person to sign this agreement would be to deny his faith, and commit a grievous sin against his children, and his God. To think of signing this form insincerely, without the intention of carrying it out, would solve nothing. Not only would one be guilty of hypocrisy and lying, but he or she would also put severe strain on the marriage when the Catholic mate came to realize that the non-Catholic mate had no intention of honoring the pledge.

The couple could decide to be married outside the Roman Catholic Church, but this procedure, too, is fraught with complications. The Catholic Church recognizes as valid only those ceremonies performed by a priest. Marriage by anyone else is not recognized by the Catholic Church, and the children born to such a union are considered to be illegitimate. If the vows are read by a minister of the gospel, the Catholic partner would also face excommunication from the Catholic Church. To say the least, such is not the way to begin a marriage!

There are so many irreconcilable differences between the teaching of the Catholic Church and the New Testament. These differences make successful marriage with a Catholic almost impossible, unless the non-Catholic mate becomes a Catholic too.

But there are other types of mixed marriages. Even marriages between two "Protestants" often lead to grave difficulties. Dehoney sums it up in these words:

Forms and practices of worship vary greatly....Some churches condemn smoking, wearing make-up, dancing, and mixed swimming as social sins or worldly pursuits while others do not. There are conflicting viewpoints toward sex even among Protestant churches. Researchers are in unanimity in discouraging young people from entering mixed marriages. They find that the difficulties of adjustment are almost insurmountable and the incidence of divorce is greatly increased. [25]

What your partner believes about religion will have a very vital influence on your marriage. Doctrines are not cold, lifeless, insignificant ideas. They have very practical consequences. For example, consider these questions:

(a) Who is God? What one believes about God determines whether the ordinary daily decisions of your marriage will be subjected to the will of God or not.

(b) What is the Bible? Is the Bible the Word of God or not? What you *both* believe about the Bible will determine whether it will be read daily in your home, privately, and to your children; and whether it will be used to give guidance to all the activities in which you engage.

(c) What is prayer? Will you be able to clasp hands as husband and wife and pray together to God, giving thanks for His blessings, and making petition for His help? Can you pray together when the baby is sick, when the husband is without a job, when you are overwhelmed by indecision, or when death is a fact? What *both* of you believe about prayer becomes very important?

(d) How do you regard Sunday? Is it to be a day of worship and church activities? Will you have to carry the full load of giving your children a religious education—all by yourself? As a wife, are you willing to do this while your husband spends his weekends on the lake or the golf

---

[25] Dehoney, *op. cit.*, p. 52.

course? As a husband, are you prepared to teach your children about God, Christ, and the Bible, without any help from your wife?

(e) What do you think about stewardship? What do *both* of you think about the Biblical command, "Upon the first day of the week, let every one of you lay by him in store as God hath prospered him" (I Cor. 16:2)? This will determine the way you allocate your money? It will determine whether there will be feelings of guilt, conflict, and hostility when you give to the Lord's work, or fail to give. Will you be able to give to the church according to a pattern that you *both* willingly accept?

(f) What about amusements? Will you agree on these? Will you be able to go together, or will you have to remain behind, because you cannot approve the activity? Or will you lower your standards so you can go together?

(g) What about your mutual friends? Who will they be? Will they be people who will have different standards from yours? Will you enjoy their association?

(h) What about the children? Which religion will they be taught? Will you permit them to be sprinkled in a denominational church? Children cannot adhere to two divergent faiths; a choice must be made. Will you let them make their own choice when they "become of age" without any effort to influence them one way or the other? Do you expect them to be able to make wise choices without any foundation upon which to make them? Or will the child be pulled in two directions at once? Will he go first with one parent and then with another? Will there be resentment between you and your mate over the religious training of the children?

What can you expect to happen to your own religious faith and convictions if you marry a person who is not a Christian? One of four things can result.

(a) You *may* lead your mate to become a New Testament

Christian. But don't count on it! A survey conducted of nearly 2000 Christians who married out of the church indicated that only about half of them were ever successful in converting their mates. [26] And then, it often took years and years. There are better and safer ways to do personal work than in marriage.

(b) You may continue in your divided state. According to the same survey, this happens over one-third of the time. In this kind of condition, many of the questions listed above become crisis points in one's marriage, and the children are constantly pulled in different directions.

(c) Both you and your mate will drop out of both churches. Authorities report that this happens about 50% of the time in Catholic-Protestant marriages. [27] When the husband and wife are of different beliefs, they tend to pull against each other and lose all interest in religion.

(d) You will be led away from the Lord's church because of your marriage partner, with you either becoming a member of his or her church, or both of you compromising on a third church. According to the survey of members of the church of Christ who married outside the church, this happened in 10% of the cases. Not only will this often result in your embracing a religion without conviction, but it may very well place your own soul in jeopardy of being lost, as well as the souls of your mate and children. It is simply too high a price to pay. Christ asked a long time ago, "What shall it profit a man, if he shall gain the whole world, and lose his own soul?" (Mark 8:36, KJV).

All of this emphasizes the fact that the time to discuss religious differences is before you take the vows to love and honor and cherish until death do you part. The question of religion must be squarely faced before you contemplate

---

[26] Batsell Barrett Baxter, "What About Marrying Outside the Church?" *Gospel Advocate.*

[27] Dehoney, *op. cit.,* p. 53.

marriage. One way to avoid the heart-breaking complications of an inter-faith marriage is simply to allow one's courtship to go no further until the question of religion is settled. But this procedure, too, is often perilous. Many instances could be cited where a young man or woman outwardly went through the form of becoming a member of the church in order to please his or her mate, and then refused to set foot inside the church building after the wedding. This, of course, is insincerity and hypocrisy of the worst sort. But it is a sad fact that it happens. This is one of the reasons we urge young people against hasty courtships. The best solution to the problem of religion is to confine dating to those who are faithful members of the Lord's church. This is the path that offers the least dangers and the surest happiness. So long as the Christian dates those who are not Christians, there is always the chance that they will fall in love, making a break painful or even impossible. It is still a safe rule to refuse to date anyone whom you would· not consider marrying.

In the New Testament there are a number of teachings which indicate that Christians should marry Christians. One of these is I Corinthians 7:12-13. Paul here presents the case of a person who has become a Christian after his marriage to an unbeliever, and he tells him not to leave the unbelieving mate. "If any brother hath an unbelieving wife, and she is content to dwell with him, let him not leave her. And the woman that hath an unbelieving husband, and he is content to dwell with her, let her not leave her husband." Now this question: If it had been a general practice in those days for believers to marry unbelievers, Christians would not have been thinking of leaving their non-Christian mates, and hence, this exhortation from Paul would not have been needed. The very fact that Paul commanded those Christians married to unbelieving mates not to leave them, indicates that some Christians were thinking they *should* leave them. In the same chapter (I Cor. 7:39), Paul commands Christian widows to marry "only in the Lord."

There is also a powerful passage in II Corinthians 6:14-18:

Be not unequally yoked with unbelievers: for what fellowship have righteousness and iniquity? or what communion hath light with darkness? And what concord hath Christ with Belial? or what portion hath a believer with an unbeliever? And what agreement hath a temple of God with idols? Wherefore, Come ye out from among them, and be ye separate, saith the Lord, and touch no unclean thing; and I will receive you, and will be to you a Father, and ye shall be to me sons and daughters, saith the Lord Almighty.

Note the three key sentences: "Be not unequally yoked with unbelievers," "Come ye out from among them, and be ye separate," and "Touch no unclean thing."

Often, concerning this passage, someone asks, "Does this mean marriage?" The answer is, "Of course, it does." Since marriage is the most intimate relationship in life, surely the principle that is taught in this passage applies to marriage. It applies equally to business, to education, or to any other type of potentially dangerous relationships.

When Paul says, "Come ye out from among them, and be ye separate," he is not meaning that the Christian married to an unbeliever is to separate from his mate. He taught just the opposite in I Cor. 7:12-13. He is simply telling Christians to come out from among the unbelievers when selecting someone with whom they will become closely yoked—in marriage, in business, in education, in recreation, or other similar endeavor.

There is sufficient evidence in the Scriptures to indicate that God expects his people to marry people of like mind. What consistency can there be in a Christian entering into such intimate relationship as marriage with one who does not share his faith in God, in Christ, in the Bible, and in the church?

The witness of both experience and the Bible warn against being "yoked together" in marriage with one who does not share the same religious faith and practice. Marry a Christian, that there be no regrets!

QUESTIONS FOR LESSON IV

1. Did your mother or father marry a Christian? If not, would they recommend that you do?

2. Discuss some of the factors involved in a Christian marrying a Catholic.

3. How could conflicting views concerning each of the following cause friction in marriage?
   (a) God
   (b) The Bible
   (c) Prayer
   (d) Church attendance
   (e) Stewardship
   (f) Amusements
   (g) Type of associates
   (h) Religious training of children.

4. Discuss four things that can happen to one's faith when he marries out of the church.

5. What are some of the dangers of dating non-Christians?

6. Do you agree that I Cor. 7:12, 13 indicates that Christians in the first century thought they should marry only Christians? Why? Does the phrase "in the Lord" (I Cor. 7:39) mean the same as "in Christ" (II Cor. 5:17)? When is one "in the Lord"?

7. What is an "unequal yoke"? Is marriage with a non-Christian an "unequal yoke"? Why?

8. Do you agree or disagree with this statement: "The real center of your married life must be in a faith that is held in common by you and your mate"?

Lesson V
ADJUSTMENTS IN MARRIAGE

If you are normal, you may expect a certain amount of conflict in your marriage. Dr. Louis M. Terman, in an analysis of 792 marriages, one of the most detailed studies of modern marriage ever conducted, concluded that even the happiest couples are not always in complete agreement with each other.[28] But some husbands and wives are in such constant conflict that "holy wedlock" has become "unholy deadlock!"

"What do you have in common?" a psychiatrist once asked a couple. The woman answered, "*One* thing: neither of us can stand the other." When John Milton's wife was once referred to as a rose, the unhappily married poet remarked, "I am no judge of flowers, but it may be so, for I feel the thorns daily." And John Wesley's wife, it is said, sat in church and made faces at him while he preached! You know you marry for better or for worse, but some may feel like the man in court who said, "But judge, she is worse than I took her for."

The idea that a bride and groom always "live happily ever after" is just simply not so. A happy marriage is the result of a great deal of hard work, and requires many adjustments on the part of both husband and wife.

One of the first things a newly married couple must learn is that their marriage is not lost just because some conflict, tension, or difference has arisen between them.

Men and women differ on a number of psychological traits. One author suggests the following comparisons as generally accepted: [29]

---

[28] Dehoney, *op. cit.,* p. 69.
[29] Alphonse H. Clemens, *Marriage and the Family* (Englewood Cliffs, N. J. Prentice-Hall, Inc., 1957), pp. 155, 156.

Men	*Women*
Men are more objective.	Women are more subjective.
Men tend to be stern.	Women tend to be tender.
Men tend to dominate.	Women are more submissive.
Men are more steady.	Women tend to moodiness.
Men are more secretive.	Women are more talkative.
Men are more impersonal.	Women are more personal.
Men think love more practical.	Women think love more romantic.

It is important that marriage partners know each other's traits, for without this knowledge, adjustment is extremely difficult, if not impossible.

In a nation-wide poll conducted by Dr. Gallup, four out of five families readily admitted having disagreements and "scraps" in their marriages. [30] And the chance is good that the other one-fifth simply had faulty memories! However, some couples "fight" more than others. Sociologists tell us that couples who fell "head over heels" in love at first sight and married after a whirlwind courtship have the most fights. On the other hand, there is much more peace in marriages where love developed gradually from friendly companionship over a longer period of time. The conclusion is that "the longer the period of courtship or engagement, the less storm and strife in the marriage." [31]

Age at marriage also makes a difference. The younger a couple is at the time of marriage, the greater the frequency of domestic free-for-alls. One author reports:

> "Couples who marry in their late teens and early twenties have the most squabbles. Those who marry in the middle twenties tend to have smoother sailing. Those who marry in their late twenties have the fewest spats of all." [32]

Authorities are in general agreement that the first seven

---

[30] Dehoney, *op. cit.*, p. 70.
[31] *Ibid.*
[32] *Ibid.*, p. 71.

years are the crucial years of a marriage. This is the period of disaster, when nearly 60% of all divorces occur.[33] If a husband and wife, during these first seven years of marriage, can meet and overcome each crisis, making the necessary adjustments in each case, and learn something from each experience, there is a good chance that the marriage will be a lasting one. Let us examine some of the common areas of conflict in marriage.

In-laws. There have been many jokes made about in-laws, and especially about mothers-in-law, but all this just points up the fact that herein is one of the major adjustments to be made in marriage. When you marry you double the number of your relatives. In marriage you are assuming a new relationship not only to the one you marry, but to his or her family as well. The Bible teaches that the relationship between husband and wife must take precedence over all other human relationships. Jesus said, "For this cause (marriage) shall a man leave his father and mother, and shall cleave to his wife" (Matt. 19:5).

Conflicts involving in-laws include matters such as where to spend Christmas, how much to spend on gifts, whether to accept loans or gifts from parents, the frequency and cost of long-distance phone calls, and how to treat free advice that is given by the parents on child-rearing, financial decisions, or a host of other subjects.

What is the solution to such conflicts? First of all, the young couple should realize that what sometimes appears to be parental interference is an expression of love and concern. Don't carry an "in-law chip" on your shoulder. And remember, that cutting the apron string is a two-way proposition. You must cut it as well as they. Resolve never to let a third party (in-laws or otherwise) come between you and your mate. But above all else, be a Christian in every test or difficulty you face. If all involved are real Christians, in-laws can be a great source of joy and real help to a happy

---

[33] *Ibid.*, p. 72.

and successful marriage. For a picture of a beautiful relationship between two young women and their mother-in-law, read the short book of Ruth in the Bible.

Nagging and faultfinding. Have you ever known a wife who was constantly irritated at her husband for leaving his shoes in the front room or his fishing tackle lying around the house? Have you ever known a husband who was always irritated at his wife because she left the top off the toothpaste or was habitually late? These are just minor irritations, but over a long period of time, they can become major issues. A frequent complaint of husbands is that their wife "nags." Webster says to "nag" is "to annoy by faultfinding; to irritate by persistent scolding or urging." A wife can keep her husband's nerves raw with endless complaints on a number of insignificant issues. It is difficult for a husband to feel real affection toward a wife who constantly nags him. Someone has said that a husband is like an egg—kept in hot water long enough he will soon become hard-boiled!

Frequently wives complain that husbands are overly critical. Nothing she does can please him. One writer tells of the wife of one hard-to-please husband who made up her mind to do her very best to please him.

> When he came in for breakfast she asked him, "Darling, what would you like to eat?" He replied, "Coffee and toast, grits and sausage, and two eggs—one scrambled and one fried." She worked hard, and soon had his breakfast on the table and called him to eat. She stood aside, waiting for a word of praise. After a quick glance, he said, "Well, if you didn't scramble the wrong egg!"[34]

How could a wife feel romantic toward such a man?

The habits of criticism and nagging are marital dynamite! They can shatter love in short order. Furthermore, the constant fault-finder is violating one of the basic teachings of

---

[34] *Ibid.*, p. 75.

Christ. Jude says "murmurers and complainers" are walking after their own lusts (Jude 16). Paul commands Christians to "do all you have to do without grumbling or arguing" (Phil. 2:14, Phillips). James says, "Do not grumble, against one another" (James 5:9, RSV). These exhortations apply to all Christians, and especially to husbands and wives. Read again Paul's description of true love in I Corinthians 13, and see how many of the traits he lists are violated by the constant faultfinder. Genuine love between husband and wife will cause them to accept their differences and adjust to any minor irritations that they may create.

Sexual adjustment. Studies show that one of the greatest single adjustments in early marriage is in the sexual realm. Dr. Oscar J. Haynes, gynecologist with the University of Louisville Medical School, says that physical sexual adjustments require an average of four to six months for most couples. [35] It is important that both the man and woman understand the physical aspects of sex, and a visit to the family physician can prove most helpful here. But this within itself will not guarantee a satisfactory sexual adjustment in marriage. More often than not, it is not a lack of knowledge about the techniques of sex, but an incomplete or unwholesome view of the place, meaning, and significance of sex in marriage that causes problems. Too, sexual maladjustment is often just a symptom of some deeper conflict between husband and wife. If most other conflicts in marriage have been handled, the problem of sexual compatibility will be minor, and will be worked out in time.

Money matters. It has been estimated that half of the arguments that arise between married couples are over money. These arguments are not usually over the amount of income, but rather, the way in which the income is spent. One researcher in Los Angeles County found a family in Beverly Hills with an income of $100,000 a year constantly involved in angry conflicts revolving around the use of that income. But in a trailor park he found a crippled man

---

[35] As quoted in *Ibid.,* p. 76.

with an arthritic wife and teen-age daughter adjusting very well to the tiny salary he made as a part-time watch repairman. On the "marriage adjustment" test the Beverly Hills family scored the lowest happiness scale and the family in the trailor had the highest score for the whole sampling of families in the county. [36]

Just as the handling of money is important in our Christian life, the proper management of money is important in the Christian marriage. One verse out of every six in Matthew, Mark, Luke, and John deal with our relationship to material things. Perhaps the following principles might be helpful for the young couple in handling their money:

(a) All the facts about family financial matters should be known equally by both husband and wife. There must be no secrets.

(b) Decisions about spending should be made together. A budget is helpful, but it must not be followed too rigidly.

(c) Both husband and wife should have some personal allowance which can be spent freely without being questioned concerning its use.

(d) An agreement should be reached about the amount to be given to the church before any other item in the budget is figured. (Cf. I Cor. 16:2; II Cor. 9:6, 7).

(e) Charge accounts should be avoided, especially in the early years. Overbuying gets many young people in trouble financially and this trouble often leads to problems at home.

(f) Make allowances for certain irrational expenditures. "The wife is going to feel she must have a new hat or a 'precious antique' once in a while no matter how many bills are unpaid, and the husband is going to buy a new golf stick or some new gadget that catches his masculine fancy. Both will make foolish purchases

---

[36] James A. Peterson, *Toward a Successful Marriage* (New York: Charles Scribner's Sons, 1960), p. 112.

and mistakes and each must understand and make allowances for it."[37]

(g) Put something away each month in a savings account—to be only for unexpected emergencies.

Remember that you can get along without nearly everything except each other. Put money in secondary place. Determine to make a *life*, not just a *living*.

Plain neglect. It is so easy to feel that once you are married, you do not have to be so careful to please your husband or wife as you were before marriage. This type of thinking sometimes breeds a neglect that is fatal to a happy marriage. Some wives think that, having "caught" a husband, it is no longer necessary to make an effort to be attractive. I remember the story of the housewife who heard the garbage truck coming just before noon and came running out of her house still dressed in her bathrobe and with her hair in curlers with no make-up. When she yelled to the driver, "Am I too late for the garbage?" he replied, "No, ma'm; jump right on."

But neglect can also come from the husband. When a wife has been home all day alone washing dishes and cleaning house, she is anxious to see her husband at the end of the working day, and to hear of all that has happened. Far too often, though, he flops down in front of the television and sits there for three hours—grumpy, silent, and moody! Such thoughtless neglect can become one of the most subtle and devastating enemies of happiness in marriage.

Children. In a normal family, the time will come when children will be given by the Lord (Psa. 127:3). Children, however, require major adjustments in marriage. They put limits on the social and recreational life of the parents. They put an added strain on family finances. We must sacrifice, and

---

[37] Adams, *op. cit.*, p. 115.

invest time, thought in them. (Read carefully Ephesians 6:1-4). But the coming of children into a home can be the stepping stone to a higher and nobler married life.

Having children is good insurance for a marriage. The divorce rate is three times as high among couples who have no children. And with the addition of each child, the divorce rate falls rapidly below the national average. [38] In times of conflict in marriage, if there are children in the home, parents simply face the conflict with greater determination to save the marriage for the sake of the children.

Immorality. There are marriage conflicts rooted in the basest kinds of immorality and sin—drunkenness, gambling, adultery, and on and on. Such problems are always difficult to solve. As has been said before, the best guarantee against them is to marry a faithful Christian, one who accepts the teaching of Christ, and abides by it. But when these types of sin occur, there is a good way out. That is through confession of the sin, and forgiveness. This requires a great deal of humility, repentance, faith, and forgiveness on the part of all concerned. In fact, every conflict in marriage can be handled by a simple application of Paul's teaching in Ephesians 4:31, 32: "Let all bitterness, and wrath, and anger, and clamor, and railing, be put away from you, with all malice: and be ye kind one to another, tenderhearted, forgiving each other, even as God also in Christ forgave you."

Dehoney lists ten commandments for the first years of marriage which will head off many conflicts. [39] They are reproduced below:

> (1) Build your marriage on a Christian foundation. Become active in church immediately after your honeymoon. Do this, not only for the spiritual guidance you will receive, but also for the company you will find there.

[38] Dehoney, *op. cit.*, p. 79.
[39] *Ibid.*, pp. 79-81.

(2) Beware of the "high-society" set or the "honky-tonk night-clubbing" crowd.

(3) Keep liquor out of your house.

(4) Start your family within the first two years. Space your children from eighteen to forty-four months apart. And look after your own children, if at all possible. Don't farm your children out to maids and caretakers or leave them with the older children.

(5) Pay a *sincere* compliment to your mate at least once a day.

(6) Go out on a date together at least once a week. Put as much effort into *keeping* as you did into *winning* your mate.

(7) Learn about the physical side of marriage. There are many reliable books in this field. Don't be ashamed to consult a competent counselor if you are having troubles.

(8) Get rid of your complexes. Grow up emotionally.

(9) Operate your home on a budget, jointly planned and executed.

(10) Bring God into your daily life. Keep a Bible at your bedside. Read it together and pray to God before you go to sleep. Thank him for the blessings of the day. Without God, your marriage will be a tragic failure. But with God's help it can be a glorious success.

QUESTIONS FOR LESSON V

1. Why do longer courtships produce more stable marriages?

2. Why would a couple with religious convictions tend to make better adjustment in marriage than those who are irreligious?

3. Constant nagging and faultfinding can ruin a marriage. How many of the traits of pure love listed by Paul in I Cor. 13 are violated by this practice?

4. Discuss each of the principles listed in the lesson for handling money in marriage.

5. Suggest some things a husband or wife can do that will help keep the "romance" in marriage.

6. How long should a couple wait after marriage to begin their family? What are the problems in starting too soon— or in waiting too long?

7. Discuss each of the ten commandments for the first years of marriage given in the lesson. Do you agree or disagree with each one?

Lesson VI

PROBLEMS IN MARRIAGE

The most important human contract on earth is the contract a man and woman make when they marry. Jesus said,

> "He that made them from the beginning made them male and female, and said, For this cause shall a man leave his father and mother, and shall cleave to his wife; and the two shall become one flesh. So that they are no more two, but one flesh. What therefore God hath joined together, let not man put asunder" (Matt. 19:4-6).

This passage tells us that God is the one that joins two people together in marriage. Marriage, then, is an agreement or a contract involving a man, a woman, and God. "What God hath joined together, let not man put asunder." A certificate of marriage is issued by the state, but the promises made are binding in the sight of God.

Many children's stories close with the words, "And they lived happily ever after." This is our desire for every young couple who marries. We hope their marriage will be both happy and permanent. But the fact is, is that every home that is established will someday be a broken home—broken by either *death* or *discord*. All understand that by death we mean the loss of either husband or wife. By discord, we have reference to such things as desertion, separation, annulment, or divorce. To realize that death will disrupt many of our happy homes is disturbing, but it is far worse to realize that many of them will be broken by discord.

There is only one honorable way for a home to break up, and that is by death of one of the partners. God intends that marriage should be for life! Paul declares this in Romans 7:2, 3:

> "For the woman that hath a husband is bound by law to the husband while he liveth; but if the husband die,

she is discharged from the law of the husband. So then if, while the husband liveth, she be joined to another man, she shall be called an adulteress: but if the husband die, she is free from the law, so that she is no adulteress, though she be joined to another man.''

He says essentially the same thing again in the Corinthian letter: ''For a wife is bound to her husband as long as he lives'' (I Cor. 7:39). Death is the only honorable way for all parties concerned, for a marriage to end. If it ends for any other cause, it will bring dishonor to one or to both of the partners. What are some of these dishonorable ways?

First, there is the matter of *desertion*. This is sometimes called the ''poor man's divorce.'' It doesn't cost anything, because one of the partners just walks off and is gone the rest of his life. Desertion is not a very pretty thing, for it is not fair to those who remain behind. It is not a legal act, but simply separation without consent of the other members of the family. There are more than 50,000 desertions every year in the United States. Usually these are among the lower income groups and certain racial groups.

In addition to desertion, which is not even as honorable as divorce, there is the matter of *separation*. This simply means that both parties enter into an agreement to live alone. The husband and wife find it difficult to live together happily, so they agree to live separately. Paul had some words to say to those who were contemplating separation:

> ''But unto the married I give charge, yea not I, but the Lord, That the wife depart not from her husband (but should she depart, let her remain unmarried, or else be reconciled to her husband): and that the husband leave not his wife.'' (I Cor. 7:10, 11).

Separation, while perhaps not a sin within itself, puts both husband and wife in a position where they are strongly tempted to fall into sin, so Paul says it should be avoided.

But in order to make the picture complete, it ought to be said that there are times when one's Christian responsibility demands that he terminate his marriage relationship. There have been instances where Christian wives were prevented from rearing their children as Christians and were prevented from performing their Christian responsibilities. As they were responsible to God, they had to step out of their marriage to a non-Christian, hindering husband. But such separation should come only when a real difficulty arises, and even then, those who separate must realize that they become especially vulnerable to sins that destroy the soul. For those who do separate under such conditions, Paul's teaching must be strictly followed: "But should she depart, let her remain unmarried, or else be reconciled to her husband."

A third method of discord of breaking up a home is that of *annulment*. Annulment is simply the declaration that the marriage relationship did not and does not exist. It is legal in civil law only when a boy and girl have not lived together as husband and wife. It may be that a ceremony has taken place, but they have not yet sustained the relationship of husband and wife through sexual union. The Bible does not use the word "annulment," and, in man's law, whenever a husband and wife have lived together, annulment is not legally possible.

As was stated in lesson one, God recognizes a marriage to be in existence when a man and woman resolve in their hearts to live together as husband and wife and when they conform to the proper civil ceremonies. The sexual union is a privilege of marriage, not a prerequisite. Hence, when two people, who are married in God's view, get an "annulment," this is the same as a divorce in God's sight, and His restrictions would apply.

The greatest concern that most of us are aware of in the area of discord in marriage is in the matter of *divorce*. Divorce is a legal decree dissolving the marriage relationship in the eyes of the state. Divorce does not depend, however, on a legal civil decree, though one should be secured if divorce is to be carried out. In God's eyes, divorce is simply the end of the sacred relationship between husband and wife. The Bible refers to the process as a "putting away."

Divorce is one of the things mentioned in the Bible that God hates. God considers the marriage vows a solemn covenant which is not to be broken. God accused some of the Jews of dealing treacherously with their wives because they put them away or "divorced" them, to take younger and more attractive wives. The first wife was called the "wife of thy covenant" (Mal. 2:14). In concluding this matter, God said: "Therefore take heed to your spirit, and let none deal treacherously against the wife of his youth. For I hate putting away, saith Jehovah, the God of Israel" (15,16). It is true that during Old Testament times, God allowed the Jews to put away or divorce their wives for several reasons. But Jesus says He allowed them to do this only because of the "hardness of their hearts" (Matt. 19:8). But "from the beginning," God has hated divorce (Matt. 19:8). And in the New Testament, Christ forbids divorce except for one reason —fornication (Matt. 19:8,9; Matt. 5:32).

The only reason given, then, in the Scriptures, for breaking up a home, other than death, is fornication. And always, in such a case, at least one of the partners stands guilty of sin, and in need of repentance and forgiveness.

In contrast to the divine plan of permanence in marriage, there is an extremely high rate of divorce in America. Our population has increased about 300% within the last 100 years; the rate of divorce has increased 2000%. In 1870, there was one divorce to every 34 marriages performed. By 1900, the figure had jumped to one divorce for every twelve marriages. In 1940, there was one divorce to every five marriages, and today there is one divorce to every four marriages in the United States. No one denies that divorce is one of our greatest national evils.[40]

Many factors have encouraged the spread of divorces, such as easy divorce laws, hasty marriages, unwillingness to make a marriage work, lack of preparation for marriage, materialis-

---

[40] Landis, *op. cit.*, p. 286.

tic pressures of our society, and, of course, a failure to consider the will of God. The real cause of every divorce is sin.

Man's laws and Christ's laws do not always agree. This is very true in the realm of reasons for divorce. Whereas Christ allowed only one reason (fornication), there are 23 reasons allowed by different states in the United States. But it is significant that "fornication" is the only reason recognized by all fifty states. Only 7 1/2% of divorces are granted legally for this reason. Forty-three per cent are granted for "cruelty," a word with all kinds of meanings; 28% for desertion; 4 1/2% for neglect to provide; and 1 1/2% for drunkenness; the remaining 15% for a large number of other causes.

There is a great discrepancy between Jesus' teaching on divorce and the teaching of society. We cannot afford to allow the world to pull us down to its standards. "Be not conformed to this world," said Paul, "but be ye transformed by the renewing of your minds." Christ allowed one reason— one reason only—for divorce. All other grounds are transgressions of His law and therefore are sinful. It may be legal to acquire a divorce for drunkenness, but it is not lawful according to the teaching of Christ. Things legal for men are not always lawful with God. It may seem reasonable to man to allow divorce on the ground of "mental cruelty," but such a divorce is not recognized by God.

It should be pointed out that although Christ *allows* divorce for the cause of fornication, fornication does not demand or compel a divorce. Fornication does not automatically break the marriage bond and no teaching of the Bible makes divorce obligatory. Divorce on the grounds of fornication is *permitted,* but it is not *commanded* or even *recommended.* God will forgive even adultery, and so should we, if the guilty party repents and requests our forgiveness, and we are able to give it. If Jesus could say to the woman taken in adultery: "Thy sins be forgiven thee. Go thy way, and sin no more," perhaps one who has the spirit of Christ may find it in his or her heart to forgive and thus save the lost, even if the lost one happens to be a husband or wife.

The evils of divorce are real, and every possible effort should be made by both parties to avoid it. Everyone suffers when there is a breakup in the home. According to one set of statistics, 50% of all divorcees regret getting divorces five years later. They admitted it was all a mistake. Thirty per cent were not certain whether it had been wise or not. Only 20% said they were "happily divorced." This ought to suggest to young people who feel tension in their homes that they ought to continue to think it over; they ought to try again and again to make their marriage succeed.

When one walks out from under marriage responsibility, he makes two grave mistakes: (a) He goes back on promises made in the hearing of God; (b) He opens himself to guilt by causing his mate to commit adultery..., "Whosoever putteth away his wfe, saving for the cause of fornication, maketh her an adulteress" (Matt. 5:32). To *cause* another to sin is to do wrong.

Death is a sad thing to come into a home, but it is not as terrible as divorce. The same beguiling serpent who brought sin into the first home in the garden of Eden is today seeking to break up every home in America. He wants to spoil every young woman and corrupt every young man. He would create suspicion, jealousy, hatred, and malice between all husbands and wives.

It is our deep conviction that only Christian principles can solve the dilemmas of the home in modern society. From no other source can two people find the needed love, wisdom, and strength to go the second mile when it becomes necessary. Only out of deep faith in Christ can we find the strength and understanding essential to marriage. Man can build a *house,* but a home must *grow.* [41]

---

[41] Much of the material in this chapter came from two sermons by Batseli Barrett Baxter, "The Broken Home," and "The Greatest Human Contract" (mimeographed).

QUESTIONS FOR LESSON VI

1. Why is desertion less honorable than divorce?

2. Is separation without divorce sinful? What are the dangers involved?

3. Why are "annulment" and "divorce" the same in God's sight?

4. Discuss the significance of the phrase, "from the beginning it hath not been so" in Matt. 19:8.

5. React to this statement: "The real cause of every divorce is sin."

6. Is divorce ever right? When?

7. What is the meaning of the phrase, "maketh her an adulteress" in Matt. 5:32?

8. Suppose a crisis arises in a home over the wife's accusation that the husband spends too much money and time on hunting trips with his friends and thus, is neglecting his wife and children. What might be the outcome of this situation:
   (a) where husband and wife are not Christians?
   (b) where husband and wife are faithful Christians?

Lesson VII
MOSES AND DIVORCE

An understanding of the teaching of the Old Testament concerning divorce will help us to understand the teaching of Christ on the subject. Thus, in this lesson we want to examine Moses' legislation on divorce among the Jews.

One of the first things that come to mind when we begin to think about Jewish family life during some periods of Old Testament times was that polygamy (a man having more than one wife) was widespread. Genesis 2:24 makes it abundantly clear that the divine ideal for marriage was that one man should have one woman for life. But in the fourth chapter of Genesis, we are introduced to the first man who violated that ideal. Genesis 4:19 says that a person by the name of Lamech "took unto him two wives." The very fact that the Bible writer specifically mentioned "two wives" shows that up until this time, which was many generations after Adam and Eve, the accepted practice was still for one man to have one woman. Lamech was the first, as far as the record shows, to turn marriage away from its divinely ordained pattern. Throughout the remainder of the Old Testament, there are numerous examples of polygamy, many of them among leaders of the Hebrew people.

Among the roll-call of well-known polygamists would be the following names: Abraham (Gen. 16:3; 25:1), Jacob (Gen. 29:23-30; 30:4-9), Elkanah, Samuel's father (I Sam. 1:1, 2), Jehoida the priest (II Chron. 24:3), Gideon, who had seventy sons (Judges 8:30; 9:2), David (II Sam. 5:13), and Solomon (I Kgs. 11:1-3). The wives of these men often were responsible for their personal backslidings and for the troubles and calamities of their reigns. Polygamy evidently became so widespread that scriptural legislation was given to control the rights of sons born to a man with two wives (Deut. 21:15-17).

Because such conditions did exist one must not assume

that they existed with God's approval. The indication is strong that polygamy was never approved by God. It is also significant that Noah, the "second father" of the human race, had only one wife. The Scriptures portray vividly some of the evils arising out of polygamy, such as jealousies of the wives contrasted to the peacefulness of marriage between one man and one woman. Kings were warned against the consequences of polygamy (Deut. 17:17). Of great significance is the fact that God's relationship with His people is always pictured as a monogamous marriage. This figure is widely used all through the Old Testament prophets as a symbol of the union of God with Israel, while polygamy represented idolatry (Hosea 2:19-23; Isa. 57:3-8; 54:5; 62:4, 5; Jer. 3:14). From all of this, it is clearly seen that the ideal of one woman for one man in marriage pervades the entire Old Testament, although God's people did not always live up to it.

Divorce and Remarriage. The Old Testament passage that contains the regulations concerning divorce is Deuteronomy 24:1-4:

> When a man taketh a wife, and marrieth her, then it shall be, if she find no favor in his eyes, because he hath found some unseemly thing in her, that he shall write her a bill of divorcement, and give it in her hand, and send her out of his house. And when she is departed out of his house, she may go, and be another man's wife. And if the latter husband hate her, and send her out of his house, or if the latter husband die, who took her to be his wife; her former husband, who sent her away may not take her again to be his wife, after that she is defiled; for that is abomination before Jehovah: and thou shalt not cause the land to sin, which Jehovah thy God giveth thee for an inheritance.

Notice that Moses permitted a man to divorce his wife if he found an "unseemly thing" in her. What does this mean? Whatever it means, we know that Moses permitted divorce and remarriage for reasons other than fornication, for when Jesus later taught that fornication was the only scriptural ground for divorce and remarriage, he was considered as teaching something different from what had been taught under the Old Law. (Read carefully Matthew 19:3-9.)

Shortly before the time of Christ, there arose two Jewish schools which clashed on the interpretation of this phrase from Deuteronomy 24. The stricter school of Shammai maintained that "some unseemly thing" meant adultery, and that a divorce could be granted only for this cause. The more liberal school, that of Hillel, argued the other extreme and placed great emphasis on the words, "if she find no favor in his eyes." This school concluded that divorce could rightfully be granted for almost any reason, even for the burning of food. Rabbi Akiba and others who followed the liberal school of thought boldly taught that "a man had a perfect right to dismiss his wife, if he found another woman he liked better, or who was more beautiful." [42] Jewish writings are filled with instructions regarding such easy divorces. Notice a paragraph from the *Talmud:*

> The following women may be divorced; She who violates the law of Moses, e.g. causes her husband to eat food which has not been tithed...She who goes out on the street, or converses (flirts) with any man, or is a noisy woman. What is a noisy woman? It is one who speaks in her own house so loud that the neighbors may hear her. [43]

Whatever the "unseemly thing" was in Deuteronomy 24, we know that it was not limited to adultery because the Law provided that a wife found guilty of adultery was to be stoned to death (Lev. 20:10).

Why were divorces permitted? Since God "hates putting away" (Mal. 2:16), it is sometimes puzzling why He allowed such a liberal law of divorce and remarriage among His people at any time during the dispensation of Moses. What was it, then, that caused this legislation on divorce to be given?

---

42 *Talmud,* "Mishna Gittim," 14:10.
43 *Ibid.*

One thing should be recognized. Though this Old Testament regulation on divorce seems to us very loose, it must be remembered that it still placed marriage on a higher moral plane than that of any of the other nations of that day. God has always required His people to live by a higher and stricter moral code than those who were not his people, and even these divorce regulations make no exception. The Egyptians, among whom the Hebrews lived for many years, had a practice of trading wives indiscriminately. The Hebrew people always had a much higher view of the sanctity of marriage and the home than did the nations around them.

Further, even this law, though allowing divorce, was framed in such a way as to discourage it. The legislation made divorce more difficult than it would have otherwise been. The law required a *written* bill of divorce; an oral statement would not suffice. To acquire a written statement calls for the help of legal authorities and the following of legal procedures. It was necessary to have at least two witnesses to the transaction, then for the husband to put the bill of divorcement actually into the hand of the woman he was divorcing; he could not have his attorney do this for him. [44] All these provisions were designed to protect the wife against being expelled from her home without due cause, and acted as a barrier to hasty divorces.

Notice, too, the stipulation in Deut. 24:4 that a divorced woman was not permitted to remarry her first husband at a later time if in the meantime she married another man. This was true even if the second husband divorced her or died, for such would have been an "abomination before Jehovah." All of this was designed to cause the husband to think seriously about divorcing his wife. He could never have her back, regardless of how much he might want her, if she remarried in the meantime. Here is further protection for the wife and children against hasty divorces. The whole purpose

---

44 Roy H. Lanier, Sr., *Marriage, Divorce and Remarriage* (York, Nebraska: Roy H. Lanier, Sr., no date), p. 53.

of Moses' law was not to *permit* divorce, but to *regulate* an evil. Divorce under Moses did not alter God's original intention concerning the permanency of marriage. When Pharisees asked Jesus why Moses had permitted them to divorce their wives, He replied, "Moses, for your hardness of heart suffered (or permitted) you to put away your wives: but from the beginning it hath not been so." (Matt. 19:8). The Jews had said that Moses *commanded* the bill of divorcement (Matt. 19:7), but Jesus put it more correctly when he said that Moses *suffered* or *permitted* them to put away their wives. And this was because of their "hardness of heart." This "hardness of heart" kept the people from coming up to the ultimate moral standard which God expects of man. Thus, Moses was only allowed to make a special concession to them for a special reason.

In Galatians 3:24, Paul tells us that the Old Law was merely a tutor or schoolmaster to bring the Jews to Christ. This means, then, that the Law of Moses was not designed to be permanent. It, and all of its regulations, were to last only until Jesus came. Today all people, Jews and Gentiles alike, must strive to live in the way acceptable to, and authorized by Christ.

The Status of Women. Under Jewish law, the divorce was always, from first to last, the husband's act. This was true mostly because the women, among the Hebrews, as among most nations of antiquity, occupied a subordinate position. The marriage relationship was looked upon largely as a business affair, though the woman was considered the husband's most valued possession. The husband was undoubtedly the head of affairs in the home, and his rights were dominant on all sides, the matter of divorce included. Though Jewish law made no provision for a woman's divorcing her husband. But when Jesus later taught concerning divorce, He made no distinction between the rights of man and woman in this matter (Mark 10:11, 12).

QUESTIONS FOR LESSON VII

1. Read Eccl. 9:9. Who wrote this? Was he a polygamist? Does this verse endorse polygamy? Why?

2. From Matt. 19:3-9, what indication is there that the Jews understood Jesus to be teaching differently on divorce than Moses had taught?

3. Discuss reasons which indicate that Deut. 24:1-4 actually *discouraged* rather than encouraged divorce.

4. What is meant by this statement? "Divorce under Moses was merely a concession."

5. Can you suggest specific ways in which Moses' regulations on divorce helped to prepare the Jews for Christ's teachings on divorce later?

6. Why does the Old Testament never speak of a woman divorcing her husband?

Lesson VIII

CHRIST AND DIVORCE

The permission to divorce granted by Moses in Old Testament times due to the hardness of the people's hearts is not granted by Christ in the New Testament.

The clearest expressions of Jesus' teaching on divorce and remarriage are recorded in the following two passages:

> And I say unto you, Whosoever shall put away his wife, except for fornication, and shall marry another, committeth adultery: and he that marrieth her when she is put away committeth adultery (Matt. 19:9).

> But I say unto you, that every one that putteth away his wife, saving for the cause of fornication, maketh her an adulteress: and whosoever shall marry her when she is put away committeth adultery (Matt. 5:32).

The teaching is plain. There is one and only one scriptural cause that can justify divorce and remarriage, and this cause is fornication. A breaking of the marriage tie for any reason other than for fornication is a transgression of God's law. Those who divorce for any reason other than fornication must either live singly or be reconciled to each other. If they contract a second marriage under these conditions, they are guilty of adultery.

Some people are bothered by the fact that in the parallel accounts of this teaching, Mark 10:2-12 and Luke 16:18, the phrase "except for fornication" is not included, but there is no real problem here. Matthew is simply giving a fuller account than either Mark or Luke. Matthew reports the Pharisees to have asked the question, "Is it lawful for a man to put away his wife *for every cause?*" while Mark records the question, "Is it lawful for a man to put away his wife?" In Matthew's account, the Pharisees had placed on Jesus a challenge to enumerate all the reasons for which a man could divorce his wife. In reply, Jesus mentioned one, and only one. Mark and Luke give only abbreviated accounts of what Matthew reports in more detail. Thus Jesus allows one reason only for divorce and remarriage—that of fornication.

What does Jesus mean by the phrase, "except for fornication"? Some have given "fornication" a very limited meaning and have said that there is no ground for divorce and remarriage exept for "an immorality which took place before marriage." They contend that fornication means illicit sexual relations on the part of an *unmarried* person only, and that Jesus would have used the word "adultery" if he had meant to include illicit sexual relations on the part of *married* persons. Now it is true that these words are defined this way in some English dictionaries, but they were not so used in the New Testament. In the original Greek, fornication is a broad term including all types of sexual immorality, including adultery. Any person (married or unmarried) can be guilty of fornication. In I Corinthians 5:1, Paul charged that there was "fornication" among the Corinthians because a young man had taken his father's wife. Here Paul used "fornication" to apply to immorality involving at least one married person. In the Scriptures "fornication" denotes "sexual immorality generally."
Fornication, then, is any sexual relationship not between husband and wife. The conclusion follows that Christ allows divorce when a spouse has engaged in a sexual relation with anyone other than his mate.

Fornication, then, is the only cause recognized by Christ which is great enough to permit one to terminate one's marriage and marry another. If a husband and wife separate for any other reason, they must either remain unmarried, or else be reconciled to each other (I Cor. 7:11).

It is contended by some that when fornication has been committed, the marriage bond is *automatically broken,* and,

---

45 William F. Arndt and F. Wilber Gingrich, trans. *A Greek-English Lexicon of the New Testament and Other Early Christian Literature* by Walter Bauer. (Chicago: University of Chicago Press, 1957), p. 700.

therefore, divorce *must* follow. The main passage cited is I Corinthians 6:16: "Or know ye not that he that is joined to a harlot is one body? for, The twain, saith he, shall become one flesh." On the basis of this scripture, the argument is made that a man becomes "one flesh" through the sexual union alone. Since, then, he is "married" to this harlot, according to this argument, the wife *must* divorce him or she will be living in a polygamous union. Those supporting this view usually do not speak of one "living in adultery," but rather as "living in polygamy."

There are several fallacies in this position. In the first place, it is clear from a casual reading of the New Testament that distinction is always made between the ideas involved in the terms "marriage" and "fornication." In the New Testament, marriage is not fornication, and fornication is not marriage. It takes something more than the act of sexual intercourse to unite a man and woman in marriage. If this were not true, then there could be no fornication as such, for all fornication would automatically become marriage. An understanding of this simple point would have answered the question of a young man who once came to my office confessing that he had committed fornication and asked, "Does this mean I'm married to that girl?"

Further, when Paul says in I Corinthians 6:16 that a man is "joined" to a harlot, he uses a Greek word for "join" which means "to cling to, associate with." [46] This word is not usually used in reference to marriage. When Paul speaks of two people being joined in marriage, he normally used another Greek word which means "to be faithfully devoted to." [47] Hence, Paul does not imply that a man is joined to a harlot in the sense of marriage, but rather he is joined in the sense that he associates with her, is in agreement with her, and in close fellowship with her. He becomes "one flesh" with a harlot in a different sense than that in which a man becomes "one flesh" with his wife. In the

---

46 *Ibid.,* p. 442.
47 *Ibid.,* p. 723.

light of the specific context and also of other New Testament teaching, the meaning of I Corinthians 6:16 must be that the man becomes "one" with the harlot in purpose and intention, lowering himself to her level both socially and as a sinner. He defiles his body, his flesh, by uniting his body with hers in the sexual act. But to say that this type of union constitutes a marriage is going beyond the teaching of the verse and of the New Testament.

It is true that the Old Testament prophecy that "the twain shall become one flesh" is quoted here in reference to *fornication* as it is in other places with reference to *marriage*. But oftentimes a prophecy may have more than one type of application, as in the prophecy, "Out of Egypt did I call my son" (Matt. 2:15). Matthew quotes this, applying it to the Christ child coming out of Egypt after the death of Herod. But in Hosea, where the original prophecy is recorded, it clearly refers to the nation of Israel, whom Jehovah through Moses led out of Egyptian bondage (Hosea 11:1). Since prophecy can have two applications, apparently the statement that says "the twain shall become one flesh" does also. It may rightfully be said that all married couples become one flesh, but not all those who are "one flesh" through intercourse alone, become married.

There is nothing in the word of God which makes divorce mandatory if a mate has been found to be unfaithful. Divorce on the ground of fornication is *permitted,* but it is nowhere *commanded* or even *recommended.* Adultery or fornication may be forgiven, but it can also be used as scriptural grounds for divorce by one who has "sincerely striven to make a success of marriage and whose redeeming love has been despised and rejected."[48] It may be wise to add that "where adultery has occurred and has been forgiven, the forgiving partner should never again present the forgiven offense as the basis for a divorce and remarriage."[49]

---

[48] Carl Spain, "Can Adultery Be Forgiven?" *20th Century Christian,* March, 1955, p. 15.
[49] J. P. Sanders, "What Does Jesus Say?" *20th Century Christian,* March. 1955, p. 9.

In every situation, the greatest desire should be that of preserving the marriage, and of avoiding divorce. But if divorce is inevitable, only the scriptural grounds may be used as its basis.

Did Paul contradict Jesus? In Romans 7:2, 3, where Paul speaks of the marriage bond, he writes that a woman is bound to a man "while he liveth;" that she is free to be married to another only after his death. He states further that "if, while the husband liveth, she be joined to another man, she shall be called an adulteress." The fact that Paul did not mention here the one exception (fornication) that Jesus mentioned, as giving one the right to remarry while his mate lived, has led some to suppose that Paul contradicted Jesus. They argue that while Christ allows divorce for fornication, Paul does not allow divorce at all. But there is no conflict. If you will read the whole seventh chapter of Romans, you will see that it is not Paul's purpose here to teach the law of Christ on divorce. He is not concerned with divorce at all. He is using the binding of the marriage law only as an illustration of the Jews' relationship to Christ. He was merely stating the rule, not discussing the exception. The rule is: Marriage shall last until death. The exception is: Fornication can break the marriage bond. The rule of God is one thing; the exception is another. The same explanation holds in regard to Paul's writing in I Corinthians 7:39. He here stated the general rule that the woman is bound for so long a time as her husband liveth. Christ's law is that the marriage relationship can be dissolved only by death of one of the mates. There is only one exception to this law—fornication. There is no contradiction between stating a general law, and yet allowing an exception. There is a law that automobiles cannot exceed the posted speed limits of 70 miles per hour. But a police car is a legal exception to this general rule. So fornication is the exception in the basic teaching of Christ concerning divorce and remarriage.

What about desertion? Some believe that in I Corinthians 7:15, Paul adds another ground for divorce and remarriage which Jesus did not include—that of desertion. Speaking of Christians married to unbelievers, Paul says: "Yet if the unbelieving departeth, let him depart: The brother or sister is not under bondage in such cases." Differences of interpretation here hinge mainly on the meaning of the word "bondage." Does Paul mean that when a Christian has been deserted by his non-Christian mate, that he is free from the marriage bond? And if so, is *desertion* another and different scriptural ground for divorce? Or, does Paul mean that if the Christian is deserted by a non-Christian mate, the Christian is not under "bondage" of obligation to try to prevent the separation, or is not under bondage to let the unbeliever dominate his life and faith?

Typical of the position taken by those who believe that this verse is not giving one the right to remarry who has been deserted by a non-believing mate is this paragraph:

> What then is the meaning of I Corinthians 7:15? ... The unbeliever refused to live with the believer, if the believer remained true to the Lord. The unbeliever would enslave the believer, would bring the believer into such abject *bondage* as to obligate him to give up Christ and finally be lost. Paul says the believer is not in such bondage to the unbeliever in order to maintain the peace of the home. If the unbeliever makes such unreasonable demands, let him depart rather than be in such bondage to him; such bondage we owe only to our Lord. [50]

Others who insist that the "bondage," from which the Christian is released in verse fifteen, is the marriage-bond point out that the context of the whole seventh chapter is concerned with the marriage relationship. This, however, does not imply that Paul had added "desertion" as a ground for divorce and remarriage.

In the city of Corinth, probably any unbeliever to whom a Christian might be married would have been a heathen, for Corinth was a heathen city. As such, a heathen married to

---

[50] Lanier, *op. cit.,* p. 27.

a Christian would have had no respect for God's teaching on divorce or on moral standards or on any other subject. One writer asks, "Could anyone suppose that such a heathen, with no ideas of Christian morality, but who because of opposition to Christian ideals deserts his partner, would live a chaste and celibate life henceforth?"[51] Desertion by such a heathen would therefore certainly include or presuppose adultery on the part of the heathen. Jesus taught that a man who puts away his wife, though she be a good moral woman, "maketh her an adulteress" (Matt. 5:32), it being necessarily understood that she will remarry. She would not become an adulteress if she remained single and chaste. Thus, Brewer concludes:

> If, therefore, it is so well understood that a woman who is put away will marry again that Christ before mentioning a second marriage declared the woman guilty of adultery, shall we not say that Paul implied that the heathen who departs breaks the marriage bond by seeking another partner of his own kind? That is most certainly understood. [52]

Another author writes: "It is probable...that in those times desertion was accompanied by adulterous or marital consorting with another person."[53]

So even those who believe that I Corinthians 7:15 teaches that desertion by an unbelieving mate frees a Christian to remarry still see that Paul allows remarriage here only on the same basis as did Christ—on the ground of adultery, presupposed if not stipulated.

The New Testament allows one, and only one reason for divorce and remarriage, and that reason is fornication. All others are out of bounds and sinful.

---

[51] G. C. Brewer, *Contending for the Faith* (Nashville: Gospel Advocate Co., 1941), p. 101.

[52] *Ibid.*

[53] John D. Davis, ed., "Marriage," *The Westminster Dictionary of the Bible* revised and rewritten by Henry S. Gehman (Philadelphia: The Westminster Press, 1944), p. 377.

QUESTIONS FOR LESSON VIII

1. Assume that A marries B. They divorce a year later for "incompatibility." Later A marries C and B marries D. In the light of Matthew 19:9 how many of these are guilty of adultery?

2. What Scriptures would you use to show that both single and married persons can commit fornication?

3. Does the New Testament endorse a "double standard" for men and women, as it relates to morals?

4. What is meant by the phrase "living in polygamy"? Is it a scriptural concept?

5. Does the New Testament teach that a person is "defiled" or "unclean" if he or she continues to live with a husband or wife who has been guilty of fornication?

6. How would you explain Paul's teaching in Romans 7: 2, 3 to someone who insists that Paul contradicts Christ in Matthew 19:9?

7. Does Paul's teaching on desertion by an unbelieving mate apply to Christians who are married to members of the so called "Christian denominations"? Why?

8. To what do you think the word "bondage" refers in I Corinthians 7:15?

Lesson IX
REMARRIAGE AFTER DIVORCE

Jesus plainly taught that any remarriage after divorce would be adulterous unless fornication was the reason for the divorce (Matt. 19:9). Those who are separated for any other reason must either remain single or be reconciled to each other. Not only does Jesus say that either party in an unscriptural divorce will be committing adultery if he or she remarries, but also that "he that marrieth her when she is put away committeth adultery" (Matt. 19:9). *All* marriages which take place after a divorce, where fornication is not the cause of the divorce, are adulterous.

In order for one to be able to remarry after a divorce, the *cause* of the divorce must have been fornication. This means that one who divorces for some reason other than fornication cannot claim the right to remarry when his divorced mate *later* remarries, for fornication was not the *cause* of the original divorce.

Sometimes it is argued that when two people divorce for some odd reason, the first one to remarry commits adultery, and then this act of adultery gives the other person the right to remarry. This is nothing more than a waiting game, to see which partner can outlast the other before giving in. Again, it must be emphasized that all marriages which take place after divorce where adultery was not the *cause* of the divorce, are adulterous. Otherwise one could get rid of an undesirable mate merely by putting them under temptation and outlasting them.

You will notice that Jesus also says in Matthew 5:32, that when a man divorces his wife for a cause other than fornication, he "maketh her an adulteress." Likewise, if a woman puts her husband away, for a cause other than fornication, it can truly be said that she makes him an adulterer. Is every divorced person an adulterer? Does the very act of putting one away make that one guilty of this sin? Certainly not. In what sense, then, does one who puts away his wife for an unscriptural cause, make her an adulteress? He makes her an adulteress by subjecting her to the temptation of remarriage or of a promiscuous sexual life. Suppose such a divorced wife has several small children and is unable to earn a living for them. She feels that she must find (and marry) someone to provide for them. Thus, she becomes guilty of adultery when she remarries, and thus her first husband "made" her an adulteress by divorcing her. Or it may be that the divorced mate is simply not able to be continent and live a pure life sexually. Paul taught that not many persons can live holy lives in the unmarried state. (See I Corinthians 7:9.) It may be that the divorced mate becomes an adulterer (or adulteress) simply because of the inability to live singly. Christ says the one who demands the divorce is guilty because it is he who has "made" her an adulteress. Every person contemplating divorce needs to consider seriously this straightforward teaching of Christ. If, as a result of an unscriptural divorce, a mate falls into an impure life, the one who demanded the divorce shall not be guiltless before God. They have made their partners guilty of adultery.

Even in a divorce with fornication as the cause, only the "innocent party" is free to remarry. Although the New Testament mentions nothing specifically concerning the remarriage of the sinful party who committed the fornication, it is obvious that he has no right to remarry. If the partners to a divorce on the ground of mere "incompatibility," where no fornication has occurred, have no right to remarry, it certainly follows that the sinful mate, the fornicator, in a scriptural divorce likewise has no right to remarry. To allow the guilty party the right of remarriage would make it more desirable to commit fornication and thus be free to remarry than to separate on other grounds where neither party could remarry. To grant the privilege of remarriage to one who has been responsible for breaking his own marriage bond would be contrary to the entire teaching of the Bible. A sinner is never allowed to profit from his sin.

But the "innocent party" in a scriptural divorce should be

very certain of his own innocence and faithfulness in rendering all the "dues of marriage" before he uses Jesus' teaching as grounds for divorce. Even when such innocence is established and there is no question as to his own fidelity, the offended party should still consider the spiritual interests of the guilty party and seek restitution and reformation if such is possible. Sanders writes: "No one whose faults in the marriage relationship constituted a contributing cause to the other person's unfaithfulness could claim to be free in such a situation." [54]

The truth is, then, that in a divorce, for a reason other than fornication, neither party is free to remarry; and if they do, they become adulterous. In a divorce granted for the reason of fornication, only the "innocent" party, if he or she has not contributed in any wise to the sin of the mate, is free to remarry.

What constitutes divorce? Why is such a second marriage adulterous? Because in the eyes of God they are still joined to their first mate. This is Paul's whole point in Romans 7:2,3. Whosoever marries a woman who has been divorced without a scriptural reason commits adultery because, in God's sight, she is still the wife of her former husband.

One must realize that the courts of the land do not have the power nor the right to dissolve a union God has made, and a man and woman may be legally divorced through the courts of the land but in God's sight still be husband and wife. Christ has stated plainly that only one cause is great enough to sever the marriage bond and allow remarriage— and that cause is fornication. Any other cause does not dissolve a marriage and does not release the parties to remarry, regardless of the decision of human courts. Albert Barnes writes: "Legislatures have no right to say that men may put away their wives for any other cause; and where there is marriage afterward, by the law of God such marriages

---

[54] Sanders, *loc. cit.*

are adulterous.[55] Any remarriage on the part of divorced persons, when their divorce was not obtained because of fornication on the part of their mate, is adultery, regardless of the civil court's decree. One author says firmly, "Adultery remains adultery even when it has been legalized." [56]

One must not, therefore, think of "divorce" merely in terms of a court action, for this is not the sense in which Jesus used the term. "The sin of destroying a marriage is in the heart and the action of the husband or of the wife (possibly in both); this is what destroys the marriage." 4 The court action and legal edict is of secondary importance and is only a subsequent result of what has already taken place in the heart and life of the couple. Because in the United States a court decree is necessary for a couple to be legally divorced in the eyes of the state, one might say that divorce in this country consists of (1) decision of the couple not to live together as husband and wife, and (2) legalization through the courts.

It would therefore be possible for a situation to exist where a couple had been legally divorced through the courts for some unscriptural reason, while at least one of the partners would still not consider the relationship broken, for it would not be broken in the eyes of God. An innocent Christian partner in a marriage could become a victim of such a circumstance, and be "divorced" by his or her mate through the courts for an unscriptural reason. He would know, however, that God does not consider the marriage dissolved, and that he is still bound to his mate. He realizes that he cannot marry another so long as the marriage bond still exists—so long as no scriptural reason for putting away his mate has occurred, and so he continues to live a chaste

55 Albert Barnes, *Notes on the New Testament—Matthew and Mark,* ed. Robert Frew (Grand Rapids: Baker Book House, 1954), p. 195.

56 Alfred Plummer, *The Gospel According to St. Luke,* of *International Critical Commentary* series (New York: Charles Scribner's Sons, no date), p. 389.

57 Richard C.H. Lenski, *The Interpretation of St. Matthew's Gospel* (Columbus, Ohio: Wartburg Press, 1956), p. 734.

and pure life (even though "divorced" by the courts), and to do everything within his power to restore his marriage. But if a restoration is impossible, and the other party later remarries, and thus commits adultery, the innocent party then has a scriptural right to terminate the marriage bond which hitherto has been binding, and is free to remarry, for now his mate has committed fornication against him. In the eyes of the State, the marriage bond was broken when the divorce decree was awarded; but in the eyes of the Lord, the marriage bond was not broken until one party committed fornication—and it did not have to be broken then, unless the innocent party saw fit. The innocent party must not "put away" (divorce) his mate until fornication on the part of the other party has occurred. Until this time, the innocent party *must* consider the marriage bond unbroken, even though the courts may have legally dissolved it. If the innocent party remarries before this occurs, he has committed adultery, and has forever forfeited his right to marriage as long as his rightful mate lives.

Is it not better to marry than to lust? Some turn to Paul's teaching in I Corinthians 7:9 ("But if they have not continency, let them marry: for it is better to marry than to burn."), and reason from this that it is better to remarry even after an unscriptual divorce than it is to remain single and lust. To make this passage teach such is to greatly misuse it. The passage is not at all concerned with the question of divorce and remarriage, but with first marriages only. Paul's advice is given to those who were thinking of leaving the single state where Paul was (not the divorced state) and entering into marriage. In no respect can this passage be applicable to one who is divorced.

What constitutes marriage? In lesson one, the principle was set forth that a marriage is recognized by God when a man and woman resolve in their hearts to live together as husband and wife, and conform to the proper civil ceremonies. It was added that if a man and woman have not made this resolve, no number of civil ceremonies can join them. There is no middle ground between marriage and adultery. Two people who are living together are either married or they are committing adultery.

Occasionally a person claims that a previous "marriage" was actually no marriage at all, and that he had no intention of living with his mate in a marriage relationship. One making such a claim must be willing to openly declare that he has been simply an avowed fornicator, living in open rebellion to the moral code of both God and the land. This is a hard statement for one to make. However, should this actually be the true situation, others could not argue that his first union was a valid "marriage" anymore than it could be argued that one who was baptized insincerely became a member of the church. In such a case, however, Brewer's advice should be taken seriously. He urges that those "trying to justify" themselves by arguing in the above manner should be "urged to be honest in striving to meet the conditions demanded by the word of God." [58]

Only in the Lord. In I Corinthians 7:39, Paul laid down a rule which is applicable to widows: "A wife is bound for so long a time as her husband liveth; but if the husband be dead, she is free to be married to whom she will; only in the Lord." If one whose marriage has been ended by death is free to remarry "only in the Lord," would not the same thing hold true for one whose marriage has ended by scriptural divorce? Widowed or scripturally divorced Christians are free to remarry, but they must marry only in the Lord—only Christians. These are God's rules.

As has been said earlier, the best guarantee for a happy life here and in the hereafter is for both you and your mate to be Christians. There would be no divorces if all people were faithful Christians.

God is the supreme judge in all cases of divorce and remarriage. His will and law must be respected. For men to tamper with God's law on this subject or any other, is to be like fools who rush in where angels fear to tread.

---

[58] Brewer, *op. cit.*, p. 81.

QUESTIONS FOR LESSON IX

1. Paul and Charlotte marry and divorce two years later for incompatibility. Neither has committed fornication against the other. Within a few months, Paul marries Alice, and Charlotte marries Jim. Who is guilty of adultery: (a) Paul (b) Charlotte (c) both Paul and Charlotte (d) Paul, Charlotte, Alice, and Jim?

2. John and Betty marry. One year later they divorce for "incompatibility." Both begin dating other people. In six months, Betty remarries. John then claims he has a scriptural right to remarry because Betty, by remarriage, has been guilty of fornication. Is John right in his reasoning?

3. Bill and Jane marry. Two years later, Jane divorces Bill for "mental cruelty." Bill tries hard to "patch things up" with Jane, but she isn't willing. After a year Bill begins dating other women and eventually remarries. Does Jane share any guilt in Bill's sin? Does Jane have a scriptural right to remarry?

4. Joe and Ann marry. They are both faithful to each other but continually quarrel. After a year, they divorce for "incompatibility." Are they still married in God's sight?

5. What is "legalized adultery"?

6. Larry and Sue marry. Later, Sue divorces Larry for "mental cruelty." Larry knows Christ's teaching on divorce and knows this is displeasing to God. Because no fornication has occurred, Larry still considers himself married to Sue though she will have nothing to do with him. He tries everything within his power to effect a reconciliation, but Sue will not cooperate. Larry continues to live a chaste, pure life, refusing to date other women. After a few months, Sue remarries. Does Larry now have scriptural grounds for remarriage?

7. If a person who is unscripturally divorced finds it impossible to live a chaste, pure life, do the scriptures give him the right to remarry even though technically this is wrong?

8. Rex and Linda, two teenagers, were out for a night of fun with some friends. In the course of the activities, someone "dared" Rex and Linda to get married by a justice of the peace that night—just for kicks. So they did. They spent one night together and then never were together again. Within a few weeks they got a divorce. Were Rex and Linda actually married in God's sight? Why?

9. Would a woman married to an alcoholic husband who beat her up every time she tried to go to church be permitted to separate from him? Could she divorce him? Could she remarry?

10. Why is this statement true? "There would be no divorces if all people were faithful Christians."

Lesson X
QUESTIONS CONCERNING CHRIST'S TEACHING ON MARRIAGE AND DIVORCE

A number of misconceptions and misunderstandings have arisen concerning the teaching of Jesus on marriage and divorce.

One such misconception is that the statements of Jesus in Matthew 5:32 and Matthew 19:9 are simply "explanations of the Law of Moses" on the subject of marriage and divorce. It is difficult to see how people can take this position if they read these statements in their contexts. It is clear in both passages that what Jesus is teaching about divorce is new and different from what had been taught by Moses. In Matthew 5:31, Jesus says, "It was said also, Whosoever shall put away his wife, let him give her a writing of divorcement." This is a reference to Moses' teaching on divorce, recorded in Deuteronomy 24:1-4. In the very next verse, Christ adds, "But I say unto you, that every one that putteth away his wife, saving for the cause of fornication, maketh her an adulteress..." "It was said" (by Moses), "but I say..." This contrast between Jesus' teaching and Moses' teaching is seen all the way through the sermon on the Mount.

For example, look at other statements in the same chapter: "Ye have heard that it was said to them of old time, Thou shalt not kill; and whosoever shall kill shall be in danger of the judgment" (a reference to Exodus 20:13 and Deut. 5:17) "but I say unto you, that every one who is angry with his brother shall be in danger of the judgment..." (Matthew 5:21,22). Jesus was teaching something deeper about anger and murder than what had been taught under the Law of Moses.

Again: "Ye have heard that it was said, Thou shalt not commit adultery" (a reference to Exodus 20:14; Deut. 5:18), "but I say unto you, that every one that looketh on a woman to lust after her hath committed adultery with her already in his heart " (Matthew 5:27,28). The first statement is from Moses—one of the ten commandments; the second is from Jesus. The second is not an explanation of the first. In giving His teaching on lust, Jesus went beyond anything that was taught in the Law of Moses.

Take one more example from the same chapter: "Ye have heard that it was said, An eye for an eye, and a tooth for a tooth" (a reference to Exodus 21:24; Lev. 24:20; Deut. 19:21), "but I say unto you, Resist not him that is evil: but whosoever smiteth thee on thy right cheek, turn to him the other also" (Matthew 5:38, 39). The Law of Moses said "an eye for an eye and a tooth for a tooth" but Jesus said, "Resist not him that is evil." Is this an explanation of what Moses taught in his law? (See * Note, Page 86).

Now, with these examples in mind, let's look again at Jesus' teaching on divorce in Matthew 5:31, 32:

> "It was said also, Whosoever shall put away his wife, let him give her a writing of divorcement; but I say unto you, that every one that putteth away his wife, saving for the cause of fornication, maketh her an adulteress: and whosoever shall marry her when she is put away committeth adultery."

Moses told the people, that if they wanted to divorce their wives, give her a "writing of divorcement." But Jesus says that if a man divorces his wife for any reason, "saving for the cause of fornication," he makes her an adulteress. Can this possibly be an explanation of the Law of Moses? If it is, then the other passages listed above must also be only explanations of the Law of Moses, because they are set in the same context.

The form of teaching in Matthew 19:9 is similar to that in Matthew 5:32. "Moses, for your hardness of heart suffered you to put away your wives ... and I say unto you, Whosoever shall put away his wife, except for fornication, and shall marry another, committeth adultery...." The Lord's disciples understood that His teaching on divorce was something different from what Moses had taught, for they said, "If the case of the man is so with his wife, it is not expedient to marry" (Matthew 19:10). Being accustomed to the freedom that was under the Law of Moses, when Jesus said they could divorce their wives only for fornication, they decided it would be better never to marry at all, than to be bound by such strict regulations. Their response to Jesus' teaching shows clearly that they knew He was not explaining the teaching of the Law of Moses.

It should not be forgotten that the Law of Moses stipulated that one guilty of adultery was to be stoned (Lev. 20). Under Moses' Law, there could not have been any "putting away" or "divorcing" of a mate guilty of fornication, because fornicators were killed, not "put away." Clearly, Jesus, in His teaching on marriage and divorce, was not simply explaining Moses' teaching.

A second false theory relating to Jesus' teaching on this subject is that since Christ's statements on divorce were not repeated by an apostle after Pentecost, they are not binding today. This theory, which actually argues that no divorces are permitted by Christ, runs like this: (1) Jesus told the apostles to teach and baptize people; (2) he told the apostles to teach the baptized to observe all things he commanded; (3) the apostles taught all that Jesus commanded, yet they did not teach that people might divorce even for the cause of fornication. Romans 7:1-6 and I Corinthians 7, are cited as the teaching of the apostles, and it is pointed out that no divorce is mentioned in these verses. The apostles taught that a woman is bound by law to her husband as long as he lives, and no exceptions were allowed.

This theory is based on the assumption that "what he (Jesus) said while in the flesh is no part of the new law, unless also set forth by the apostles." But this assumption is not right, and therefore, the conclusion is not right. Take, for example, what Jesus taught us about the way to treat a brother who has sinned against us. He said,

> "And if thy brother sin against thee, go, show him his fault between thee and him alone: if he hear thee, thou hast gained thy brother. But if he hear thee not, take with thee one or two more, that at the mouth of two witnesses or three every word may be established. And if he refuse to hear them, tell it unto the church: and if he refuse to hear the church also, let him be unto thee as the Gentile and the publican " (Matthew 18:15-17).

Where did an apostle ever teach this procedure? This is the only place in the Bible where such a procedure is taught, and yet all people admit that it is the rule to be followed by the church.

Jesus lived and died under the Law of Moses. The old Law was not "fulfilled" or "taken away" until He died on the cross (Col. 2:14). But Jesus taught many things during His personal ministry which were meant to be applied after His church had been established—after Pentecost, and until the end of time.

Take another example. In Matthew 5:28, Jesus says, "Everyone that looketh on a woman to lust after her hath committed adultery with her already in his heart." Where did an apostle ever teach this? The apostle John taught that if we hate a brother we are guilty of murder (I John 3:15), but no apostle ever taught that we are guilty of adultery if we lust after another. Does the teaching, therefore, not apply to us?

There are many other examples that could be cited, such as Jesus' teaching, "Call no man father" (Matt. 23:9), which was never repeated by an apostle. Are the Catholics, therefore, justified in their practice of calling the priest "Father"? Is this teaching of Jesus' not applicable today?

One author points out that if Jesus' teaching on divorce and remarriage is not now in force, then it never was and never will be, and therefore, is a useless and idle statement.

"It was not in force during the law of Moses which lasted until the death of Jesus. It will not be in force in the next world, for there they neither marry nor or given in marriage (Matthew 22:30). If this part of the statement of Jesus is not in force from his death (or Pentecost) until the end of time, it never was and never will be in force, so an idle statement." [59]

A major item of disagreement among Christians has to do with whether Christ's marriage law applies to non-Christians. If it does not, then there is no sin involved in an unscriptural marriage contracted by non-Christians. If it does, then the mâtter must be considered further. Those who say that Christ's laws on marriage and divorce apply to all people (Christians and non-Christians alike) point out that sin is defined in the Bible as "the transgression of the law" (I John 3:4, KJV) and that Paul says, "where there is no law, neither is there transgression" (Romans 4:15). If the non-Christian is not responsible to any law, then there never could be any sin. Yet the Scriptures say, "all have sinned" (Romans 3:23). If the alien (non-Christian) is not subject to the law of God, it would not be possible for him to sin since sin is transgression of law. If there is no *law* condemning an *act,* it would be no sin. Hence, aliens without law cannot be sinners and would not need to be baptized for a "remission of sins" (Acts 2:38). This would also make absurd the preaching of the gospel and urging people who have no sins to be baptized to wash away their sins (Acts 22:16).

Those agreeing with this conclusion point out that although Gentiles were never under the Law of Moses, when Christ died on the cross, ushering a new law into effect, both Jews and Gentiles were obligated to that new law. The gospel, the New Testament, is addressed to all people, both Jews and Gentiles, both Christians and non-Christians, and every person who violates the teachings of this new law will be held accountable before God. The teachings of Christ

[59] Roy H. Lanier, Sr., "Divorce and Remarriage," *Firm Foundation,* Dec. 1, 1964, p. 769.

are addressed to everyone: "Go ye into all the world, and preach the gospel to the whole creation" (Mark 16:15). Fornication, murder, lying, stealing, etc., are sin for any-one, because Christ's law declares them to be sin and all people are responsible to this law. They contend that simply because one does not happen to *know* that stealing is sin does not excuse him from that sin. The same, they say, would be true for murder, lying, adultery, etc. They conclude that if Christ's law does not apply to non-Chris-tians, then they can engage freely in murder, lying, steal-ing, adultery, etc. without the penalty of sin for "where there is no law, neither is there transgression" (Romans 4:15).

Those taking the position that non-Christians are not controlled by Christ's marriage law contend that the only sin of which a non-Christian is guilty is the sin of unbe-lief. Those outside of Christ, we are told are lost already and therefore are not subject to God's law and cannot be guilty of any *specific* sins. They contend that the teaching of Jesus in the moral realm was intended for his disciples only. According to this view, the sinner's sole responsibility to God is to accept Jesus and obey the gospel.

But those taking the opposite view are quick to point out that Ananias commanded Paul, as a non-Christian, to "arise and be baptized, and wash away thy sins" ("sins" in the plural) (Acts 22:16). Furthermore, they point to such passages as I Corinthians 6:9-11 where Paul said members of the church at Corinth had been fornicators, drunkards, thieves, idolaters, covetous, etc. before their conversion, but that they were "washed" and "justified." If they were guilty of these specific sins before baptism, then Christ's moral law must have been binding on them. In answer to this, however, some claim that it was only the civil law that these Corinthians had violated prior to their con-version and not God's law. They say these people had violated the law of the land which forbade these things. But here again, the point is raised that some of the sins in this list could not possibly have been prohibited by civil

– 85 –

law in Corinth. Fornication, for example, was not a violation of the state law in Corinth, for it was practiced in religious temples as part of worship to pagan gods. Covetousness is also in the list, and no state has ever passed a law against that sin. Idolatry is also listed, yet Corinth was noted for its worship of state-sponsored idolatry would not have been against the civil law. It is insisted, therefore, that it was God's law that was violated by these pagan Corinthians, and not just the civil law. They point out that the conclusion must be that when a non-Christian violates the moral law of Christ today, he has sinned just as surely as these Corinthians had, and is in need of a "washing" through baptism of these sins.

Related to the view that Christ's moral teachings do not apply to the non-Christian, is the view that God does not recognize the marriages of non-Christians. The position of those holding this view is that there can be no unscriptural divorce among non-Christians bécause God has not recognized their marriages in the first place. "Marriages are made in heaven," we are told, and if neither partner to a marriage is a Christian, God takes no account of their union. Those differing with this concept point out that this doctrine has ugly implications, because it would mean that all children born to non-Christian parents are illegitimate. It is insisted that Christ's law concerning marriage is a universal law, meant to apply to all people in the world. [60]

*It may be that in the Sermon of the Mount, Jesus is contrasting his teaching more with the perverted interpretations of the scribes and Pharisees than he is with the Law of Moses itself. (See Allen C. Isbell, *War and Conscience*, Appendix 1, Biblical Research Press). However, it is clear that in his teaching on divorce, Jesus was not teaching the same thing as Moses had, but was going back beyond Moses to the way God had wanted it "from the beginning."

---

[60] Much of the material in this chapter was taken from the tract by Roy H. Lanier, Sr., *Marriage, Divorce and Remarriage* (York, Nebraska: Roy H. Lanier, Sr., no date.)

QUESTIONS FOR LESSON X

1. Read from your Bible the passages listed below from both the Old Testament and the New Testament on each subject listed. Discuss the Contrasts!

KILLING	Exodus 20:13 Deuteronomy 5:17	Matthew 5:21, 22
ADULTERY	Exodus 20:14 Deuteronomy 5:18	Matthew 5:27, 28
SWEARING	Leviticus 19:12 Numbers 30:2 Deuteronomy 23:21	Matthew 5:33, 34
RETALIATION	Exodus 21:24 Leviticus 24:20 Deuteronomy 19:21	Matthew 5:38, 39
DIVORCE	Deuteronomy 24:1-4	Matthew 5:31, 32

2. List as many of the teachings of Jesus as you can which were not repeated by an apostle after Christ's death. Are these teachings binding today?

3. Evaluate this statement: "If Christ's teaching on divorce is not in force now, it has never been and will never be, so it is just an idle statement."

4. Do you think Christ's teaching on divorce applies to all people or just to Christians? Why?

5. What do you think of the argument that the only sin of which a non-Christian is guilty is the sin of unbelief? How do Acts 22:16 and I Cor. 6:9-11 relate to this?

Lesson XI
STATUS OF THOSE DIVORCED
BEFORE BAPTISM

There is a great deal of confusion in the church today concerning what those must do who have sinned in regard to God's law on divorce and remarriage. The question is: If one has divorced unscripturally and has remarried, what must he do in order to repent and make his life right with God? There is very little confusion among church leaders concerning the answer to this question when it involves people who are baptized believers. Should a Christian divorce his wife, without the claim of fornication, and contemplate remarriage, most congregations would enforce Christ's rule which states he has no right to do so. Or if a Christian is contemplating marrying one who is divorced from her mate without a scriptural reason, most churches would insist that he not take that step, realizing it would be a transgression of Christ's law. If the Christian persisted in his intentions, discipline would be exercised, and the Christian would have to cease living with his unlawful mate, in order to be restored to recognition as a faithful child of God. Certainly this is the procedure that should be followed, for the couple is living in an adulterous relationship as long as such a "marriage" prevails.

The controversy becomes heated, however, when one considers the question of the status of people who have divorced and remarried without scriptural cause before they became Christians. The situation might be presented as follows: Two non-religious people marry, but later divorce for a cause not recognized by the law of Christ. Later one of them remarries, lives for years together with his second mate and has a family. Finally they hear the gospel of Christ preached and decide to obey it. They learn for the first time that their present union is adulterous. What must these people do? Will baptism wash away all their past sins, and also leave them free to continue in their present relationship, or must they, in order to repent, dissolve the adulterous union and separate from each other? This focuses the problem.

The first question that invariably arises is the one discussed in the last lesson: Do Christ's moral teachings, including His teaching on divorce and remarriage, apply to the people in the world—to non-Christians? If they do not, then there is no sin involved in the unscriptural marriage contracted by non-Christians. But if Christ's teachings do apply to them, we must face the problem. If people "in the world" sin when they violate God's laws concerning divorce and remarriage, what is required of them when they repent in order to become Christians? Must those joined in an unscriptural marriage in God's eyes separate, or are they free to continue that relationship?

Some contend that, since all sins are forgiven at baptism, one is free to continue to live with whatever mate he has at the time, regardless of the number of unscriptural divorces which preceded his marriage. One author in replying to the question, "Must those who have been unscripturally divorced and remarried before baptism, separate to make it right, or to be forgiven?" writes:

> Paul says the scriptures furnish us thoroughly unto every good work. Paul's scriptures answer this question. He says, 'Be not deceived, neither fornicators, nor idolaters, nor adulterers.... And such were some of you: but ye were washed, but ye are sanctified, but ye were justified in the name of the Lord Jesus Christ, and in the Spirit of our God' (I Corinthians 6:9-11). Two answers are offered by men. You may pick your own according to which is the scriptural one: (1) Must adulterers separate before being baptized? Man answers: 'Such were some of you: but ye put away your wives, ye sanctified yourselves, ye justified yourselves.' (2) Must adulterers separate before being baptized? Paul answers: 'Such were some of you: but ye were washed, but ye were sanctified, but ye were justified in the name of the Lord Jesus Christ, and in the Spirit of our God.' If salvation is by works of righteousness which we have done (Titus 3:5), the first answer is correct. If salvation is by grace, and sins are washed away in baptism, the second is correct. Some

in the church at Corinth had been adulterers. Paul didn't say they separated. Paul says they were washed, sanctified, and justified in the name of the Lord Jesus Christ, and in the Spirit of our God. [61]

The same author goes on to say:

> One is raised from the grave of baptism to walk in newness of life—all things are made new. The past is erased and sins all forgiven... Every glance backward only reminds him of God's mercy and grace. He is not to dwell on the mistakes of the past. Forgetting the things behind he is to press toward the mark of the high calling of God, in Christ Jesus... The terrible sins of the past are forgiven in baptism, by the grace of God. [62]

But others insist that the question is not whether all sins are forgiven in baptism, but rather, whether any of them are licensed for continuation. All admit, they contend, that baptism washes away all sins including adultery, for the one who is truly repentant. But is one who has obeyed the gospel free to keep on living in an adulterous union after his baptism? One author writes:

> Suppose a man is living in polygamy, and he decides to obey the Gospel. May he continue to live with a dozen wives after his repentance and baptism? Does his obedience to these commandments of the gospel change his polygamy from unholy relations to holy relations? Polygamy is one form of adultery; living with a person who has been divorced from another for any cause except fornication is another form of adultery. If one may continue to live in one form of adultery after repentance and be pleasing to God, why may he not live in the other form of adultery after repentance and be pleasing to God? Repentance means that one ceases to live in sin. The thief quits stealing when he repents; the drunkard quits his drunkenness when he repents; the polygamist gives up his plurality of wives when he repents; and the one

[61] J. Luther Dabney, *Dabney-Frost Debate* (Cullman, Alabama: Gene Frost, 1959). p. 15.
[62] *Ibid.*, pp. 20, 21.

living in adultery with a divorcee must dissolve his adulterous union. [63]

Replying directly to the argument that in I Corinthians 6:9-11, Paul did not say these fornicators separated from their mates, but rather that they were "washed," one writer points out:

> Whatever is said of the adulterer is said of the idolater, thief, and drunkard. Neither does I Corinthians 6:9-11 specifically state that they put away the idol, robberies, or the bottle. Are we then to conclude that one may sin before baptism, be baptized with no intention of ceasing sin, and continue to commit the sin of idolatry, theft, drunkenness with impunity and God's favor? If this is true of adultery, it is true of the other sins in the same text and the same relationship! [64]

The real question that is at the heart of this issue is: What is involved in repentance when those who have divorced and remarried unscripturally obey the gospel?

Some contend that the sin of those in unscriptural marriages is the fact that they divorced their first mates without a scriptural reason. Therefore, all that these persons must do in order to repent is to resolve never to divorce unscripturally again. They must resolve to "stop forming adulterous unions." But, others point out that, though a sin was committed when an unscriptural divorce was obtained, that this is not the *only* sin involved. They refer to Jesus' statement in Matthew 19:9: "Whosoever shall put away his wife, except for fornication, and shall marry another, committeth adultery." They conclude, therefore, that the committing of adultery in an unscriptural marriage is sin just as much as the obtaining of the original divorce, and that both sins must be repented of. The parties involved must resolve not only to quit divorcing unscriptur-

---

[63] Lanier, *Marriage, Divorce and Remarriage,* p. 18.
[64] Gene Frost, *Davney-Frost Debate* (Cullman, Alabama: Gene Frost, 1959), pp. 25, 26.

ally, but also to quit committing adultery. Those holding this view emphasize the fact that the Greek verb, *moikatai,* which is translated "committeth adultery" in Matthew 19:9 is in the present tense which indicates continuing action (as versus "one time" action). Thus: "Jesus is saying, literally, that when one divorces and remarries another without the cause of fornication he keeps on committing adultery as long as the marriage relationship exists. Baptism will not change this, only repentance will, and repentance demands that we put away sin."[65] The same writer said earlier:

> "Adultery is an act! It is an illicit sex relation and as long as that relation is continued one continues to be guilty of adultery. How can the very act which is adultery before baptism become all right after baptism? Baptism does not make a sin become righteousness!"[66]

However, some make a strong contention that the relationship of adulterers is changed in baptism so that illicit sexual acts are not illicit. The Scriptures cited in support of this position are Romans 4:7-8 and I Corinthians 6:9-11. In Romans 4 Paul quotes from Psalm 32 these words: "Blessed is the man to whom the Lord will not reckon sin." In I Corinthians 6:9-11, after stating that fornicators, idolaters, adulterers, thieves, drunkards, etc., shall not inherit the kingdom of God, Paul adds: "And such were some of you: but ye were washed, but ye were sanctified, but ye were justified in the name of the Lord Jesus Christ..." The conclusion some draw from these passages is that

> when the sin is not imputed, and the adulterer is justified, the adulterous marriage becomes an approved one. ...Since the sin is not imputed to adulterers after baptism, they do not have to separate from their wives, because marriage of the just and righteous is not a sin....When an adulterer is righteous and acceptable to God, he is

---

65 Charles A. Whitmire, "What About God's Marriage Law?" *Firm Foundation,* Nov. 17, 1964, p. 733.
66 *Ibid.*

no longer a sinner... When forgiven of adultery, his marriage in the sight of God is just as acceptable as that of any other righteous and just man. [67]

Others, however, differ strongly with this interpretation. Consider, for example, the following:

When one divorces for trivial cause and marries again, he enters an unholy union. The union is unholy in God's sight because God holds him bound to his first partner. Divorce for any cause other than fornication does not destroy the union in God's sight. What God joined, no man can put asunder. Since God joins a man to his first lawful wife, and since divorce for trivial cause does not destroy that union, if the man marries again he is living with one woman while bound to another. That is what makes the second union unholy. Does baptism change the nature of that union? Does baptism cause an unholy union to become holy? Can the polygamist continue to live with six wives after his baptism for the remission of sins? Can the 'confidence artist' continue conning people after his baptism? If baptism will make an unholy union holy, why won't it make an unholy *occupation* holy? [68]

"God will forgive adulterers, but He will not permit them to continue in a state of which he has just forgiven them. If so, this is the only unscriptural relationship in the world which is changed by repentance and baptism from a sin into a grace." [69]

Persons who insist that adulterous unions must be dissolved at baptism usually are careful to point out that while repentance does carry with it the idea of restitution, of making things right as much as it is within one's power to do so (Luke 19:8; Matthew 21:28-30), it is not always possible to make restitution for sins already committed. If a thief steals a large amount of money and spends it before he becomes a Christian, it may be impossible for him to pay the money back. Furthermore, they point out, in many

---

[67] Dabney, *op. cit.,* pp. 103, 93, 95.
[68] Lanier, "Divorce and Remarriage," p. 769.
[69] Willeford, "Repentance and Unscriptural Marriages," p. 18.

cases of unscriptural marriages, it may be impossible for the people involved to go back and be reunited with their lawful companions. They insist, however, that though the thief may not be able to restore the money he has stolen, he still must cease to steal, and though the one involved in an unscriptural marriage may not be able to return to his first mate, he can still cease to live in an adulterous relationship.

Often it is pointed out that nowhere in the New Testament do we have an example of a man giving up unholy marital relations when he became a Christian. In answer to this, it is said that we need no example of this, "because repentance was placed before baptism, and its meaning was so clear that all sinners knew they had to quit all unlawful relationships and practices." [70]

I Corinthians 7:20 is often used by some to support the position that a person is to keep living with whatever companion he has at the time of his conversion. The verse says: "Let each man abide in that calling wherein he was called." It is pointed out that in verse 27, Paul adds: "Art thou bound to a wife? Seek not to be loosed." Thus: "This admonition includes marriage. If not marriages contracted before baptism, what?" [71] Others, however, reply that in this passage Paul is speaking only of those relationships which are holy within themselves; not of unholy ones. He is speaking of a first marriage, or of one's social background (slave, master, Jew, Gentile, etc.), but not of a state or "calling" of adultery.

A very common objection to the view that people unscripturally married must separate at the time they become Christians, is that this will entail hardship and suffering on the part of any innocent children that may have been born to that union. Attempting to answer the objection, one preacher writes:

---

[70] *Ibid.,* pp. 17, 18.
[71] Dabney, *op. cit.,* p. 17.

"It has been ever true that sin brings suffering, not only on the sinner, but upon those who are involved on account of various relationships to the sinner. But shall we shut our eyes to sin because some innocent person is about to be hurt? Shall we declare sin is no longer sin if any innocent party is about to suffer?" [72]

Another adds:

"Sympathy for children affected by their parents' sin does not alter God's law. No one denies that correcting sin will often entail many hardships, but the blessings of peace with God far outweigh them. Jesus said, 'He that loveth son or daughter more than me is not worthy of me' (Matthew 10:37). If sympathy for those who must make sacrifice in order to obey the Lord will allow one to disregard his law on marriage, then it will allow one to disregard his law on baptism, worship attendance, self-denial, or any other of his commands." [73]

Another objection often raised to the idea of dissolving unscriptural unions is that "one of the mates may not be able to live a pure life" under such an arrangement. But a reply is that, while it may be difficult, it is not impossible, for the Lord requires *separated couples* to live that way (I Corinthians 7:19-21).

May God help each one of us to be sincere seekers of the truth on this subject as well as on all others. May He aid us in prayerfully considering His will. Truly, the problem of marriage and divorce is one of the thorniest problems confronting members of the church of the Lord. A great deal of wisdom and help from the Lord will be required to work through it.

---

72 Willeford, "Repentance and Unscriptural Marriages," p. 18.
73 Bill Minick, Jr., *Questions and Answers on Marriage and Divorce,* tract (Quinlan, Texas: Just a Moment Publishing Co., no date).

QUESTIONS FOR LESSON XI

1. Why is the word "marriage" in quotation marks in the last sentence of the first paragraph of this lesson?

2. In your mind, is there a conflict between teaching that all past sins are forgiven in baptism and also teaching that a couple living in an unscriptural marriage at the time of their baptism must separate? How would you deal with the polygamist or the thief?

3. *Why* do some insist that when one who is unscripturally divorced and remarried repents and becomes a Christian that he and his mate must separate?

4. What is the significance of the Greek verb translated "committeth adultery" in Matthew 19:9?

5. In your opinion, does baptism change an adulterous union into a holy one? Why?

6. To what extent does God expect one who has violated His law on marriage and divorce to "make restitution"?

7. Do you think the argument that "nowhere does the New Testament contain an example of a man giving up an unholy union when he became a Christian" is valid? Why?

8. Do you think I Corinthians 7:20 applies to the problem under discussion in this lesson?

9. What do you think of the arguments concerning the hardships that children suffer when an unscriptural marriage is dissolved?

10. Is it possible for one separated from his spouse to live a pure, chaste life?

Lesson XII

AFTER DIVORCE WHAT?

Divorce has been called "the unhappy opposite of a wedding." This is an apt statement, for the wedding is the legal, official beginning of a marriage, and weddings are traditionally happy occasions. Divorce is the legal seal that officially ends a marriage, and divorces are not happy occasions. Divorce is very seldom the *solution* of anything. It is rather a retreat, an attempt to escape from a problem situation. One of the natural questions in the minds of many divorced persons a few years—or even a few months— after the decree is: "Which was the greater failure, my marriage or my divorce?"

The time to take a good straight look at divorce is before you marry. An understanding of the real nature of divorce will encourage you to choose your mate more carefully and wisely. You will go into marriage with a stronger determination to build for success. You will know ahead of time that, once married, the task is to work through any problems that arise, because divorce is no easy way out.

Many people have the same, or similar, problems in their marriages. Some marriages with big problems end in divorce, but some do not. What is the difference? The group which does not end in divorce has one essential ingredient: a determination on the part of both to hold the marriage together. Some marriages seem to hold together in spite of elements contributing to failure, because the couple are not willing to resort to escape or retreat.

It cannot be denied that divorce is much more common today than it was a generation ago. There are several factors which have contributed to the rising divorce rate. One writer says: "Modern marriage is like a tent, the stakes of which have been pulled out one by one, each time making it more vulnerable to wind and storm."[74]

---

[74] Henry A. Bowman, *Marriage for Moderns,* 4th ed. (New York: McGraw-Hill, 1960), p. 511.

People often speak of the "gay divorcee." Actually, however, there is no glamour to divorce. The best that can be said is that some newly divorced people are forced to put on a gay face for the benefit of their watching friends, at a time when their hearts are filled with pain and regret or bitterness. In the typical divorce case there are two persons whose dreams have fallen in ruins.

Many divorcees have later learned that by divorcing, they were jumping from the frying pan into the fire. It did not solve their problems. It was not a solution, but was merely an escape. Many admit later that they really loved their mate more than they realized, that the situation was not so bad after all, that the divorce was too hasty, and the decree is regrettable. Summarizing the effects of divorce on the mates, one sociologist writes:

> The divorced person faces several acute problems. He must settle the conflict and rebellion within himself. He must repair wounded pride. He must readjust his habits. Often he does not realize until he is called upon to change them how much a part of his life many habits have come to be. He must reorganize his social relationship with his children, whether he is separated from them or has them with him without the other parent. He must reorient his sexual life. If the person left alone by divorce is a woman, she must usually arrange for support. [75]

Authorities in the field of marriage and divorce enumerate several serious problems that come to most divorcees. Each of these tends to underscore the futility of divorce. What are some of these problems?

(a) *Feeling of emptiness.* Marriage is a very intimate relationship, and it simply is impossible to end such a relationship as this without sensing a loss. When the lives of two persons become interwoven, it is difficult to separate them without leaving in each mate a serious emotional problem. Even two people who do not get along very well together still become

---

[75] *Ibid.,* p. 518.

more dependent upon each other emotionally than they may realize. It is often a very serious emotional shock to try to adjust again to living as a single person, alone, after having been married.

(b) *Feeling of remorse.* Doubts often arise in the divorcee's mind about the wisdom of having taken such a serious step. Often this is accompanied by a feeling of regret—a feeling that he or she should have worked harder to make the marriage last.

(c) *Self-accusation.* Often the divorcee wonders if he or she has been too self-centered; if he or she should have practiced more of what Christ taught about a willingness to sacrifice. After all, the marriage vows were a promise "for better or for worse." Guilt feelings arise.

(d) *Feeling of defeat.* When one goes through a divorce, he has admitted publicly that, regardless of the reasons, he was simply incapable of making a success of his marriage. Getting married was a public announcement of the belief in one's ability to achieve happiness with a certain mate, and divorce is an open admission of failure. There is a loss of face, of prestige, for just as there was pride in the ability to gain a mate for marriage, so now there is now a feeling of humiliation at having lost one.

(e) *Reliving the past.* Marriage, even a marriage that is not particularly a happy one, has a way of becoming part of an individual, part of his life, part of his personality. Memories of courtship days and the early years of marriage cannot be easily erased. Such memories lead to moods of depression.

(f) *Bitterness.* When one realizes all that he has lost as a result of divorce, there may be a reaction of intense bitterness against one's former husband or wife who agreed to the divorce. There may also be bitterness against friends and relatives who did not put forth more effort to stop the procedure.

(g) *Self-pity.* A divorced person may think of himself as just a victim of circumstances which he could not control. The result may be a feeling of persecution and intense self-pity. Many times, no matter how depressed and inwardly hurt a divorced person may be, he may try to put up a bold front and an "I-don't-care" attitude. As one woman expressed, "If he had died, people would grieve with me. He is gone: but people only look at me and expect me to go on as if nothing had happened. I can't even admit that I grieve."[76]

(h) *Feeling of isolation.* Divorce may issue in feelings of loneliness and isolation, due to the change in one's social life. New friends, for the most part, must be found, and new interests must be cultivated. The divorcee often feels like a "fifth wheel" for whom there is no place in social groups. What is to be done about mutual friends which both mates had before divorce? To associate with them as a single person seems unnatural and awkward. This feeling of isolation is especially pronounced for the woman.

(i) *Marriage on the "rebound."* In spite of Christ's teaching concerning remarriage after divorce, there is often a strong tendency to "save face," especially on the part of the mate unwillingly divorced by the other. He or she may rush into a new marriage to prove that he or she has an adequate and desirable personality. Studies indicate that about one-half of all divorced persons do remarry, and that there is a strong tendency for divorced persons to marry other divorced persons. This, of course, has serious implications in view of Jesus' teaching on remarriage after divorce. "Whosoever shall put away his wife, except for fornication, shall marry another, committeth adultery: and he that marrieth her when she is put away committeth adultery " (Matthew 19:9). Divorcees are not the best prospects for successful new mates.

(j) *Financial problems.* Divorce creates or increases financial

---

[76] Landis, *op. cit.,* p. 296.

problems, especially for the woman. She must now plan for her own support. Even if alimony is paid, it is seldom sufficient to allow freedom from financial worries. She may have to find employment in order to meet her expenses. For the wife without previous work experience, or for the wife with small children this is a formidable problem.

(k) *Unnatural attitude toward children.* In divorces where small children are involved, additional problems present themselves. Who shall be given custody of the children? Shall the children remain continuously with one parent or shall they be shifted from one parent to the other? If a separation from one's children, either temporarily or permanently, becomes necessary as a result of divorce, this is often the most heartbreaking experience of all. The writer knows a young man, a member of the Lord's church, who is ruining his life through drinking and other sinful activities, because of the deep void he feels as a result of a divorce which took from him his only child.

In addition to all the effects of divorce upon the mates, there are also the effects of divorce upon the children. While divorce may be the choice of two unhappy parents, it is almost always painful for the children. The child so often loses his feeling of security, and his efforts to achieve peace within himself and to accept the situation is usually accompanied by a great deal of emotional turmoil.

One author- describes the effect of divorce on children in the following words:

> "The child of divorced parents is in a position somewhat akin to that of the middle horse in a three-horse team, which is pulled now in one direction, now in another, now in both at once, as it attempts to accommodate itself to the movements of the other two horses. The child is torn between conflicting loyalties. He tries to cooperate with and to understand two persons who are at odds and do not understand each other. If he lives with each of them at different times, he is pulled first

one way, then another. In neither home is he prepared for living in the other."[77]

Suppose that your parents have just informed you that they are contemplating getting a divorce. Assuming that this announcement comes as a surprise to you, what would your reaction be? You may have sensed that their marriage was not "perfect," but you never dreamed that a divorce was in the making. You are confused and you begin to worry. You lie awake at night. You cannot study. You seem to feel that life is constantly pressing in upon you. Your security seems threatened. You had always taken the world in which you live for granted; it was the foundation of many things in life about which you felt sure. But now it is about to collapse. What can you do?

We should not be surprised when those who have been through the ordeal of divorce urge others not to follow in their steps.

A faithful Christian lady, who has been divorced for some years, writes the following statement about divorce, and her divorce in particular.

"I had been reared in a Christian home and the idea of *my* divorce had never entered my thinking. In conversation with others I had often made the statement, "I'll never get a divorce; the only reason people ever get a divorce is to be able to remarry." The greatest shock I ever faced in my life was when I realized there was little choice. After wrestling alone with my problem for too long, I sought counsel from our elders who had known me from my youth. (My husband refused to attend any counselling sessions with me). Our elders told me they felt I had a scriptural reason for divorce. Even at this point, I'm sure I would not have gone ahead with the divorce if there had not been the question of child custody and property settlement involved. Several months later I sat in the lawyer's chair still thinking this must be someone else, answered a few questions and then the simple legal procedure was over. Making a new life for my family now meant many changes from the former plans. Getting employment was the easiest task because my profession was much in demand and I felt secure in that area. But many ideas and plans had to be discarded. In fact, it

---

[77] Bowman, *op. cit.*, pp. 518, 519.

was necessary to go in debt for the necessities sometimes. One of my constant fears was who would care for my family if I should become disabled. For this reason I made more expensive and more elaborate plans than the average parent would need to make. Perhaps the one hurt most felt by a divorced woman that is least obvious to those around her is that of 'not belonging.' There are so few places I can go where I feel I really fit in. Any small social group which involves a few friends has no place for me. The group of widows which seems to be the most likely group usually includes several older women with grown children. I'm interested in being with parents who have children the age of mine and likewise similar problems. My fear, too, is that I might hold on to my family too tight and too long. That out of loyalty to me their own lives might be affected in making a life of their own. What of the future? Growing old alone is dreaded by all. Many couples discuss the possibility of growing old alone but with me I'm attempting to make definite plans for it. The only thought I've been able to entertain that offers any comfort at all is the one hope and prayer that has sustained me through all of this. That hope is my knowledge that God will help me to bear my burdens. That prayer is that I may be able to live only one day at a time and live that day to the fullest in the work of God's Kingdom. To any young person who feels divorce is the solution to your problem, I would say explore every other alternative before turning to divorce. Remember God has given only one reason for obtaining a divorce and even when a marriage is ended for this cause, one must face a long and lonesome life after divorce. There are many, many problems which one never anticipates and which you will have to face alone after the divorce." [78]

Can you see now more clearly why divorce has been called "the unhappy opposite of a wedding"? Talk to those who are divorced, and you can see how really unhappy it is

"Most marriages are happy. Even those couples who divorce, often find that they were far happier while they were married, and they regret their divorce. The sound attitude is to choose a mate wisely and then go into marriage ready to accept the responsibility for creating happiness. Success or failure is largely within the individual." [79]

[78] Personal letter to the author.

[79] Landis, *op. cit.*, p. 298.

QUESTIONS FOR LESSON XII

1. Why is divorce more of a "retreat" than a "solution"?

2. Why do divorcees often feel an "emptiness" after divorce?

3. Do you think one can ever be sure in his own mind that he did all he could to save his marriage?

4. In what respect is divorce an open admission of failure?

5. Why does a divorcee often become bitter?

6. Are others normally more sympathetic with one whose mate has died or one who has lost a mate through divorce?

7. Why does a divorcee tend to feel isolated socially?

8. Why do you suppose divorcees tend to marry divorcees? What are the scriptural implications here?

9. What do you think is the most serious effect of divorce upon children?

10. What is meant by the statement: "Success or failure (in marriage) is largely within the individual"?

Lesson XIII

BUILDING A PURE AND HAPPY LIFE

The chances are that, if your marriage is truly a successful one, your entire life will be successful and happy. Most marriages can and do succeed. As a matter of fact, almost any marriage can succeed if both parties really want it to, and if each is able and willing to do his part physically, emotionally, and spiritually. Both must be ready to take the help of God and the church, and to profit from the experience of others.

The most essential element for a pure and happy life is pure and genuine love between a husband and wife. Paul, in Ephesians 5, writes a powerful passage describing the relationship to two people in a happy, Christian marriage:

> "You wives must learn to adapt yourselves to your husbands, as you submit yourselves to the Lord, for the husband is the 'head' of the wife in the same way that Christ is the head of the Church and saviour of his body. The willing subjection of the Church of Christ should be reproduced in the submission of wives to their husbands. But, remember, this means that the husband must give his wife the same sort of love that Christ gave to the Church, when he sacrificed himself for her...Men ought to give their wives the love they naturally have for their own bodies. The love a man gives his wife is the extending of his love for himself to enfold her...The marriage relationship is doubtless a great mystery...In practice that I have said amounts to this: let every one of you who is a husband love his wife as he loves himself, and let the wife reverence her husband." (Eph. 5:22-23, Phillips translation.)

In this passage, the togetherness that must characterize a husband and wife is called "a great mystery," meaning that only those who are mature enough will be capable of seeing and understanding this "great mystery." Sometimes it is said that marriage is a 50-50 proposition. But this is not taught in the Scriptures. Does the passage in Ephesians

5 indicate that marriage is a 50-50 relationship? Isn't it more of a 100-100 relationship? The husband is to "love his wife as he loves himself." How much love is this—50%, 90%, 100%? In Titus 2:4-5, Paul says that young women are to be taught to love their husbands and to love their children, to be kind and obedient to their own husbands. Does this sound like a 50% proposition? A 50-50 marriage is doomed to failure. It is only the 100-100 marriage that will be pure, happy, and successful.

Selfishness is at the root of almost every problem in marriage. Sometimes other things such as ignorance and immaturity are involved, but the fundamental problem of all marriage problems is selfishness. Let us look once more at Paul's description of true love in I Corinthians 13.

Nothing can destroy a marriage if this kind of love fills the heart of both partners—

> "Love suffereth long" ("Love is patient"—RSV)
> "Love is kind"
> "Love envieth not" ("Love is not jealous"—RSV)
> "Love vaunteth not itself" ("Love is not boastful"—RSV)
> "Love is not puffed up" ("Love is not conceited"—NEB)
> "Love doth not behave itself unseemly" ("Love is not rude"—RSV)
> "Love seeketh not its own" ("Love does not insist upon its own way"—RSV)
> "Love is not provoked" ("Love is not touchy"—Phillips)
> "Love taketh not account of evil" ("Love keeps no score of wrongs"—NEB)
> "Love rejoiceth not in unrighteousness" ("Love does not gloat over other men's sins"—NEB)
> "Love rejoiceth with the truth" ("Love delights in the truth"—NEB)
> "Love beareth all things" ("There is nothing love cannot face"—NEB)
> "Love believeth all things" ("There is no end to its trust"—Phillips)
> "Love hopeth all things"
> "Love endureth all things" ("Love can outlast anything"—Phillips)

Kenneth I. Brown has written a book entitled *Margie*. It is about a Christian young lady who wrote to the boy she planned to marry:

> "I love you not only for what you are but for what I am when I am with you. I love you not only for what you have made of yourself but for what you are making of me. You have done it without a touch, without a word, without a sign; you have done it by being yourself. I guess that is what being a sweetheart really means."[80]

This is love at its highest and best.

Research has indicated that even the happiest married couples are not constantly in complete agreement. In a normal marriage, even if Christian, there will be a certain amount of conflict. Someone has said that marriage is like buying a phonograph record—to get what you want you have to take what's on the other side. In other words, the most ideal person has faults. Marriage does not eliminate them. These faults often cause irritations and conflicts in marriage. But in a Christian marriage, the mates are able to see that beneath the surface feelings are deeper feelings of real and genuine love, and hence they are able to work together in overcoming these conflicts and in assuring their own happiness.

Dehoney gives some excellent suggestions in a chapter of his book entitled, "How to Quarrel Constructively."[81] He suggests several positive ways to handle conflicts when they arise in marriage:

(a) *Try to understand the other person.* Is he or she tired or ill? Are there tensions or pressures? Try to deal with what is causing the conflict rather than the conflict itself.

"A keen observer says that one of the daily highlights

---

80 As quoted in Adams, *op. cit.,* pp. 60, 61.
81 Dehoney, *op. cit.,* pp. 93-103.

for the dogs in his neighborhood is the delivery of the morning paper. They come charging out at the paper boy with violent outbursts of barking that would frighten the bravest man. However, the shrewd paper boy never retaliates with rocks or kicks. In fact, he doesn't even scold them. Instead, with soft kind words, he calls them to him and pets them. This action always stops the barking. It magically changes the savage beasts into warm friends. The paper boy is smart enough to know that most of the time when a dog barks ferociously he is actually revealing his own fear and insecurity. Deep down he wants to be petted and appreciated. When a husband 'barks' at his wife, or the other way around, it often merely means, 'Honey, I'm tired and things didn't go well today. Please, pet me a little.' Or, the irritable one may be saying in this devious way, 'I'm worried about the outgo that exceeds my income. Love me and make me feel a little more secure.' "[82]

(b) *Try to understand yourself.* Why are you annoyed? Is there something that is causing you to be upset? What is it? One author tells of a couple who wisely agreed on a warning signal to the other when they did not feel their best. Whenever the wife was out of sorts, felt irritable, and had a hard day at home, she would greet her husband in the evening with her apron turned inside out. When he had an especially tiring day at work, and his nerves were raw and on edge, he came home with his hat brim turned down. Each noticed the signal and acted accordingly. As we understand ourselves, we can go a long way toward helping others to understand us, too.

(c) *Talk it out.* Husbands and wives must learn to express themselves freely to each other. They need to have times when they can discuss the things that are upsetting them. In these sessions, they can often find ways to resolve petty grievances before they become big ones. There must, of course, be a spirit of good will and of give-and-take. And once a problem is resolved, it should be forgotten. A man said, "While we were arguing, my wife got historical."

---

[82] *Ibid.,* pp. 97, 98.

The friend said, "No, you mean she got hysterical." "No, I mean historical—she brought up everything that I had ever done wrong in my life." A good memory is a blessing, but sometimes a good "forgetter" is even a greater asset.

(d) *Attack the problem* instead of each other. One of the hardest things in the world is to control one's tongue when he is angry. Words uttered in anger will usually attack each other rather than the problem, and will leave deep-seated scars. It is never wise to discuss differences when tempers are hot.

(e) *Hold on to* the concept of unconditional *togetherness.* You can expect to disagree frequently but you can resolve to love continually. One woman tells of how she and her husband lost everything during the depression. They had to leave their luxurious apartment for a simple home with few conveniences. The first night in their new home she turned to him, somewhat overcome, and said with a sigh, "Well, we're *here*!" He turned with a smile, put his hand in hers and said, "My dear, the important thing is, *we're* here!" This kind of partnership; this kind of love and understanding can bring good out of what would otherwise seem to be an evil day.

(f) *"Let not the sun go down upon your wrath"* (Eph. 4:26). Psychologists say that children have a natural ability to forgive and forget. They can fight one minute and be friends the next. But somewhere along the way, adults lose this talent. Could it be because we forget that we, and our mates, are just ordinary people, with many virtues, but also with many faults? True love—as well as true forgiveness—means accepting ourselves and our mates as we are—a combination of virtues and defects.

When Paul commands us not to let the sun go down on our wrath, he is simply urging us not to let our hostilities pile up from day to day. He is telling us that, before we go to sleep each night, we should clear away all anger and resentment from our hearts; confess, forgive, and express our love toward each other. At times the three words, "I am sorry" can be the most important words you can utter. The inability to say, "I am sorry" has broken up many homes that otherwise could have been saved. There is so much at stake: your happiness on earth, and perhaps your eternal destiny. "Learn to say 'I am sorry,' and then live in harmony with the apology. Learn to forgive and to ask forgiveness. Having a quarrel can rend your heart, but making up can be a wonderful experience." [83] All of this really amounts to nothing more than a practical application of the golden rule and the counsel of Paul in Ephesians 4:31, 32;

> "Let there be no more resentment, no more anger or temper, no more violent self-assertiveness, no more slander and no more malicious remarks. Be kind to one another; be understanding. Be as ready to forgive others as God for Christ's sake has forgiven you." (Phillips translation.)

To all these suggestions, let's add one other: Give Christ and spiritual values a prominent place in your home. The most essential element in any home is God. If both husband and wife are sincerely striving to follow the teachings of Jesus Christ, the marriage will be pure and happy. Worship God, not only at the appointed times of public worship, but worship together in your own home with your children—daily. Pray together. Study the Bible together. At the very beginning of your married life, make a commitment to Jesus Christ, and fulfill that commitment. Dr. John L. Hill during his life as an educator and civic leader, never accepted an appointment or responsibility that involved Wednesday night. He always replied that he had a previous engagement. He attended prayer meeting. When a family establishes the principle of putting first things first (Matt. 6:33), it does not leave the family calendar open to weekly debate about attending worship services. Only a full-fledged commitment to Christ and His church will provide an adequate foundation to insure a marriage against all the elements

---

[83] Thomas B. Warren, *Marriage is for Those Who Love God and One Another* (Fort Worth: Warren Publications, 1962), p. 130.

that tend to destroy it. A family clinic in Nashville, Tennessee, designed to help those who are having difficulties in their marriage, reported that there had not been a couple before the clinic who had attended church together during the previous two years.[84] One writer says that when counseling a husband and wife who are having trouble, he challenges them to promise each other that for at least thirty days they will *together* read the Bible for at least fifteen minutes, and that they will pray together, holding the hands of each other, after they have gone to bed at night.[85] He says if they will do this honestly and sincerely, he has absolutely no doubt as to what the outcome will be.

From all that has been said, it can be seen that the real key to a pure and happy life is a spiritual one, and that a husband and wife can build an enduring marriage only as they learn to genuinely experience love, acceptance, and forgiveness of themselves, of each other, and of God.

The marriage decision is the second most deeply serious one you will make during your lifetime. There is only one other decision that is so important—and that is your decision to give your life to Christ. This decision should be made first, even before seeking out a marriage partner.

May God help each of you to put into practice in your own lives the truths and concepts you have learned in this study. May He help you to build pure, happy, Christian homes. May you never forget that when God joins two people in marriage, they are joined for life.

Whom you marry may very well determine where you spend eternity. Take all the spiritual training that is available. Learn God's Word and the inexhaustible wisdom that it contains. Have the courage to wait until you are fully grown to take this serious step. Do not take another into your life until you have taken Jesus Christ as your Saviour and King!

---

[84] *Nashville Tennessean* Magazine, May 1, 1960.
[85] Warren, *op. cit.,* p. 143.

QUESTIONS FOR LESSON XIII

1. What is meant by the statement that marriage is not a 50-50 proposition, but rather a 100-100 relationship?

2. Do you agree with the statement in the lesson that selfishness is at the root of almost every marriage problem? Why?

3. Give an illustration of how each characteristic of love mentioned in I Corinthians 13 could help toward building a happy marriage. Discuss the characteristics one by one.

4. Is it realistic for two Christians to expect to have no conflicts in their marriage? Why?

5. Discuss each of the suggestions made by Dehoney for "quarreling constructively."

6. Do you agree with this statement: "If both husband and wife are sincerely striving to follow the teachings of Christ, their marriage will be pure and happy"?

7. What is meant by the statement that the real key to a pure and happy life is a spiritual one?

8. What is the greatest single concept that you have gained from this study which you feel will be the most helpful to you in future years?